QUIET LESSONS FOR THE INTROVERT'S SOUL

QUIET LESSONS FOR THE INTROVERT'S SOUL

GABRIELA CASINEANU

Formatting, Cover Design: Gabriela Casineanu
Images: Johannes Plenio (pixabay), Presenter Media

Editing: Christina Friend-Johnston

Library and Archives Canada Cataloguing in Publication

Casineanu, Gabriela, 1961—, author

ISBN: 978-1-9994249-4-7 Paperback
ISBN: 978-1-9994249-5-4 Hardcover
ISBN: 978-1-9994249-3-0 Electronic Format
ISBN: 978-1-9994249-2-3 Electronic Format (K)

To be yourself in a world that is constantly trying to make you something else is the greatest accomplishment.

— RALPH WALDO EMERSON

CONTENTS

I dedicate this book to…

• The 11 brave introverts—Mimi, Alex, Mihaela, Gerard, Carol, Charles, Louisa, Adina, Louise, Petros, and Liliana—who opened their hearts and shared their stories, holding a mirror for us to learn more about introversion. Thank you!
• My readers, friends, and acquaintances who—through their comments —helped me understand the need for a book like this. Thank you!

And to …
• The curious introverts who are willing to learn more about themselves and their strengths by reflecting on the content of this book;
• The extroverts who are open to better understanding the introverts in their life, their struggles, and strengths;
• Those who don't know where they are on the extroversion-introversion spectrum, but are interested to find out;
• The parents of introverted children who would like to learn more about the rich inner world of their children, and how to create a nurturing and supporting environment that make them flourish as adults.

~ Gabriela

DISCLAIMER

Although the author and publisher have made every effort to ensure that the information in this book was correct at press time, the author and publisher do not assume and hereby disclaim any liability to any party for any loss, damage, or disruption caused by errors or omissions, whether such errors or omissions result from negligence, accident, or any other cause.

Adherence to all applicable laws and regulations is the sole responsibility of the reader. Neither the author nor the publisher assumes any responsibility or liability whatsoever on behalf of the reader of this material. Any perceived slight of any individual or organization is purely unintentional.

This book does not replace counseling, professional coaching, or therapy. The information and resources in this book are provided for informational and educational purposes.

Whenever a gender-specific term was used, it should be

FOREWORD

What can I say? I absolutely love this book!

I especially treasure the author's takeaways at the end of each interview. As an introvert myself, I can identify with so many! I so appreciate how she made the connections between what has been said and how this applies to other introverts as a whole.

The lessons learned in this book have brought forth an even greater appreciation to being someone who often turns her thoughts inward, seeking quiet moments to refuel.

These valuable chapters of exploration help us understand, appreciate and further develop our own unique strengths.

What a true gift this book is, both to introverts as well as those seeking to learn more about them.

Eevi Jones
Founder of Children's Book University, Publishing Strategist

WHAT READERS SAY

about Gabriela's books

Quiet Lessons for the Introvert's Soul

I found this book life transforming. The list of positive attributes for introverts is ENORMOUS! Embrace being an introvert; it's cool, it's hip and the author is educating us all about our (hidden?) talents. A game changer for me!

~ Amazon customer

I learned that I can be my quiet self while I pursue my dreams, without having to pretend to be someone I'm not. Highly recommend this book!

~ Petros Eshetu

I love that the author tracked down introverts to interview and got them to open up. As it turns out, introverts have some AMAZING qualities! Just because they need some breathing room at times doesn't mean they are stupid or unfriendly. They have some lovable quirks and are pretty smart!

~ LMB Amazon Customer

Introverts: Leverage Your Strengths
for an Effective Job Search
(Readers' Favorite Award Winner, International Bestseller)

After reading this book, I feel like I have been given a secret key to success, so I can do things my way as an introvert while not stretching too far out of my comfort zone (or maybe more if I like!), and still be respected and even sought after for my skills.

~ StaceyK

I've got a contract! As a Business Program Manager, I'll jump in and help get a project straightened out—this is perfect for me! I'll step out of the technical side and get closer to management consulting (what I want). So your idea career as a journey—each job should be taken only if it brings you closer to your goal—actually works! I've been recommending your book to just about everyone!!

~ A.B.

Taken to heart, this is a book that will open your eyes to how you can create new opportunities by changing your own approach and align it with your strengths. It is written with care, experience and research and stands out with pearls of details to help you to where you decide to go!

~ Amazon Customer

Meeting With My Self:
Self-Coaching Questions That Invite the Wisdom In
(Photo-Coaching Book 1)
(International Bestseller, featured in Amazon Prime Program)

As a psychologist I feel very fortunate to have found this unique and inspiring book, not only for my clients but for myself. The beautiful photos invoke emotional and intellectual responses. The questions lead to insights and ah ha moments.

~ Amazon Customer

Among the self-help books that crowd today's marketplace, I found "Meeting with Myself" to be exceptionally moving and inspirational. For me, this book has the deeply moving simplicity of a Japanese Zen garden. In 40 pages, it inspires readers to explore their own unanswered questions in fresh, stimulating ways, and act on what they discover. This book deserves the Zen Buddhist applause of a single hand clapping!

~ E. Thomas Behr, PhD

Navigating the Relationship Landscape
(Photo-Coaching Book 2)

A wonderful tool for gaining clarity about relationship issues and reach a deeper understanding of the people you care about and want to relate to at your best.. Reflecting on the photos helps cut through the noise and confusion and get right to the heart of the matter: how can we get along best with those we love? It's hard to think of any other method that can provide this level of clarity and insight in such a short time.

~ Rebecca C.

I love this book on relationships! So simple and yet so profound. I liked the innovative style of linking beautiful photography with minimal script. As a former professional psychologist, both in education and in employment, I do feel this book is to be treasured in many situations because of its potential for everyone and anyone.

~ Evelyn S.

The Key Factor: Understanding the Employer's Perspective on Hiring

As a career coach myself, I know how frequently job seekers get so wrapped up in themselves that they miss fundamental steps in marketing themselves. This concise read helps job seekers to see the bigger picture. It offers strategies to communicate with employers and invaluable tips to increase your chances of success.

~ S. Peppercorn

A must read for those the individuals who are willing to go on an adventure to discovering their best "self" to present to employers.

~ D.M.G.

Job Fairs: How to Get the Most of Your Participation

I used to think that finding a good employer at a job fair was like trying to find a good romantic partner at a bar—in other words, the meet-market that leads nowhere good. This book has done what few books can do: it offers a different and much more positive perspective AND a sensible, workable plan.

~ Jacquelyn Elnor Johnson

This book is a must-read for anyone looking for a job at a job fair, whether just graduating or multiple job fair attendee.

~ Carole Nap

HOW THIS BOOK CAME TO LIFE

Soon after I published my first book *(Introverts: Leverage Your Strengths for an Effective Job Search)*, many readers reached out to me sharing how much that book helped them understand themselves better. Some confessed that before reading that book they were not even aware they are introverts! This made me think that many other introverts might not be aware of all their strengths and how to use them!

I've also met people who consider themselves as extroverts or ambiverts just because in some situations they are energetic and talkative. Well, this can happen to introverts if they're in good company or talking about something meaningful to them!

Initially, I thought of writing a book about the differences between introverts and extroverts, but eventually I got a better idea: to interview only introverts for this book!

After all, having introverts' stories about how they overcame some of their challenges is more interesting and useful (in my opinion) than reading a book that just presents introverts' and extroverts' characteristics.

You're about to embark on a journey of discovering how 11 interviewees used their introvert strengths. I hope that you'll also be surprised by how much YOU resonate with most of their struggles and get inspired on how to use your introvert strengths better!

I certainly did! :-) In this book, I mentioned some of my memories that were triggered by hearing their stories as an invitation to help you do the same: reflect on your own life and figure out how to use more YOUR strengths!

If you're familiar with introvert characteristics, you know that introverts don't like to talk about themselves, especially about their private life! Including me, I'm an introvert too.

"So, how did you find introverts who opened up and shared their challenges with the world?" you might wonder.

Well, I tapped into some of the introvert strengths of the interviewees…and mine! :-)

First of all, since this is a meaningful project for me, I dared to ask who would like to be a part of this book project. While we (introverts) usually struggle with asking for what we want, if it's about a meaningful cause we get a motivational boost to do it! And 11 introverts answered my call.

Second, I was able to connect with them and build trust by being genuine (one of the introvert's strengths).

And third, even if you build trust and ask introverts to share their own stories, there are slim chances to get an affirmative answer unless you tap into another introvert strength: we like to help people! So when they heard there's a project that has the potential to help many other people —especially other introverts like them—I've got their attention!

I also needed to give them time to digest my request.

A couple of months after I asked, someone sent me a message: "I just realized that I am such an introvert that I didn't even have the courage to reply to your invitation for an interview. If it's not too late, I'll say yes now." Well, it was not too late! :-)

Let me say a big THANK YOU to all these introverts who opened their heart and shared their touching stories with us!!! You'll find their coordinates at the end of this book. What's interesting: they live or lived in various countries around the world (US, Canada, UK, Italy, Romania, Lebanon, UAE, South Africa, Zimbabwe, Ethiopia, Australia, Argentina, and Japan).

In some interviews, I had to put on my coaching hat and ask questions to help them bring their stories to the surface. We're so accustomed to our life that sometimes we don't even realize what power our stories could have on others! Do you?

Please let me share this: with almost every story I heard through these interviews, I've had goosebumps at one point or another. Which means to me that we're on to something big here—bigger than those who participated in this book project! There's certainly a *sensitive fabric* underlining these stories that resonate with us, but maybe not in the same way (depending on our own journey). Each of these stories seems like the *Hero's Journey* about a specific aspect of an introvert's life—the *Introverted Hero's Journey*…if I may say!

I'm both humbled and honored to be *chosen* to bring this

book to the world, to help introverts understand themselves better and how they too can overcome their challenges!

I dare to say that even extroverts will benefit from reading this book. They'll become more aware of the power and rich inner world of the introverts present in their lives! And this increased awareness will help them to infuse more positivity and empathy in their personal and professional relationships! After all, introverts and extroverts might be like the *Yin and Yang* of humankind! They have complementary strengths to create a better world for all of us!

Here's something that I found surprising while conducting these interviews: even if the interviewees were aware of their introverted nature, some were not entirely aware of their introvert strengths…or how these strengths played a role in overcoming their challenges.

We don't usually reflect on our past experiences, do we? And even if we do, are we really looking to spot our strengths and the role they played so we can use them even more in the future?

Toward the end of each chapter, I pointed out some of the introvert strengths that showed up in those stories and some examples.

Although many of these strengths show up in several stories (if not in all), I didn't point out all the strengths that I noticed in each story for two reasons: I didn't want to make the chapters longer, and I wanted to entice YOU to spot those not listed! :-)

My purpose with this book is to provide you with an enriching and useful experience, besides reading interesting stories about introverts' challenges.

That was my experience with this book and my wish for YOU too! I even got a few "AHAs" myself while interviewing these wonderful introverts, and even after (while reviewing these interviews).

The way I structured this book is an invitation for you—the reader—to redirect your focus back (toward your own life) at the end of each chapter and reflect on what you can learn from these stories and introvert strengths...to apply to your own life from now on!

Warning: if you're not used to self-reflection, reading these stories might be easier and faster than reflecting on how these lessons could positively influence your life!

I just couldn't help myself to not put on my coaching hat while I brought together the different pieces of this book. I have to walk my talk, right? :-)

Toward the end, you'll find a chapter with two of my life's challenges and what helped me to get through them. I thought it would only be fair that I too open up, not just ask others to do it! This idea came up while reviewing these interviews, realizing how generous these introverts were to open up their hearts allowing us to get a glimpse into their lives and struggles!

If you're curious to identify introvert strengths while reading all these stories—or just to keep it as a reminder—you can download the **List of Introverts' Strengths** covered in this book: gabrielacasineanu.com/list-introverts-strengths

While reading these stories, you'll probably feel like you're sitting comfortably in a café, sipping your coffee (or tea) while overhearing the discussions at a table nearby!

LIST OF INTROVERTS' STRENGTHS

covered in this book

Curious about what introvert strengths helped the interviewees overcome the challenges shared in their stories?

Download the **List of Introverts' Strengths** and keep it handy while reading! (4-pages PDF file)

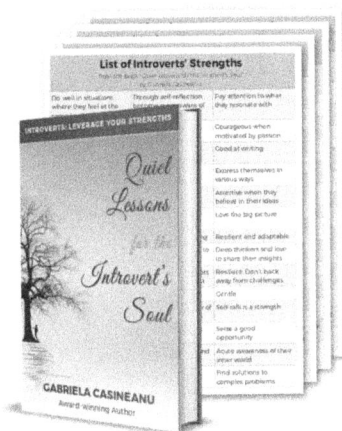

WHY THIS BOOK TITLE?

Since introverts are perceived as quiet people, I consider the lessons learned from these introverted interviewees as *quiet lessons*. Also, based on my experience with this book—and of those who read it so far—the book content *quietly* triggers insights into the readers' mind.

The real stories about how these introverts overcame their challenges touched my introvert soul deeply. These stories highlight a broader perspective of the rich inner world of introverts—and what they're capable of—which is less known in a society where extroverts are more visible.

Whether you're an introvert or extrovert, I hope that this book will touch your soul too! :-)

HOW TO USE THIS BOOK

Feel free to skip this section if you're not interested in my suggestions on how to use this book. :-)

As I mentioned earlier, I planned the structure of this book is a way that gives you an experience, so you can learn more about yourself and how to enjoy more your life.

You'll find below how I envision you the use of this book, followed by a few other suggestions.

How I envision the use of this book

• Have a notebook and pen handy

• Download the **List of Introverts' Strengths** from here:

gabrielacasineanu.com/list-introverts-strengths

• Start with chapter 1 *(Mimi)* because it gives you more information about the introverts' characteristics backed by science. Then you can read the following chapters in any order you want. Just make sure you read them all because each interview brings new useful *tools* and *techniques*.

• While going through each chapter:

1. Pay attention to what resonates with you and which of your memories are triggered
2. Write in the notebook a few words about these, you'll come back to them later
3. Read my comments about the introvert strengths I've noticed in that interview
4. Look at the *List of Introverts' Strengths* to see if you discover other strengths in the same interview
5. Write down any new insights you've got by going through the previous two points
6. Reflect on your notes.

• Read the last two sections (after the chapters 1-12), as they contain additional information, and go through the exercises as well. Write down and reflect on the new insights you get.

• Decide what you'd like to do based on your notes and the experience with the whole book.

• And, of course, start taking those actions. :-)

• If you're inclined to: leave an honest review on Amazon, to help others better understand what the book is about and if it might be beneficial to them too.

Other ways to use this book

1) Download the *List of Introverts' Strengths* and keep it handy while you read any of the chapters 1 to 12. Identify which of those strengths were used in each story. Identify what

strengths you have that are similar to the interviewee's and how you can use them more in your own life.

2) Read a chapter at a time and reflect on it for a couple of days. Notice what you resonate with, what memories come to the surface, what new insights you get, and what actions you'd like to take (write them down). Then move on to the next chapter.

3) Read the book without taking any notes and reflect on the whole experience at the end. Then, if you want, look at the *List of Introverts' Strengths* and put a checkmark near each strength you identify in yourself. Think of one or two of your experiences that exemplify each of those strengths.

Since there are too many strengths to memorize, post this checklist in your room or office as a reminder. These strengths are *tools* that you can tap into at any time, to be proactive and overcome challenges more easily.

4) Whatever way you choose to *navigate* through the chapters, read the last two sections (*My Takeaways* … and *Now…Your Turn*). I'm pretty sure you'll find something valuable there too.

My intention with this book is to help introverts understand that they're on a journey (*Introvert's Hero Journey*). While each of our journeys is unique, there are *tools* and *techniques* that we can use along the way to make our journeys more enjoyable.

I don't think any of the interviewees will have a problem if we borrow some or all of their *tools* and *techniques*.

That's probably why they shared them with us! :-)

QUIET LESSONS FOR THE INTROVERT'S SOUL

Chapter One

MIMI

It was like a rebirth pretty much because at various times it looked as if I would die and I didn't. So to me, I'm really living in Bonus Time now.

— MIMI EMMANUEL

While Mimi lives in Australia, I met her through a Facebook group for authors while I was writing my first book. She was already a bestselling author, so I trusted the generous advice she shared with me. That evolved into quick chats via private messages, and I credit her for encouraging me to continue writing and publishing books. Thanks, Mimi!

In one of those chats, I mentioned my idea of writing this book, without knowing that she's an introvert. Not only did she like it but—as a *100 percent introvert* (as she calls herself)—she accepted to join this book project!

We often hear that introverts don't like to talk. Well, I'm here to tell you that when two introverts find the time to talk about things they consider important and meaningful, that saying is definitely not true! :-)

What we thought would be a 30-45 minute interview, ended up being almost two hours! The discussion touched upon so many interesting topics that I kept most of them, thinking that you might find them useful as well. So this is the longest interview you'll find in this book.

Now have your favorite *cuppa*,* and tune in to the vivid discussion I had with Mimi!

Australian for "have a cup of tea" or "have a cup of coffee"

Gabriela: Mimi, please share with us some of the biggest challenges you had in life and how you were able to overcome them. What did you do? What beliefs and attitudes helped you overcome those challenges?

Mimi: First, let me say that you are the person who opened my eyes in regards to being an introvert or an extrovert. I've never given it a lot of thought, but then I read your first book, *Introverts: Leverage Your Strengths for an Effective Job Search*, and I thought: "I'm definitely an introvert, without a shadow of a doubt!"

Gabriela: That's interesting! I love when people tell me that my first book helped them realize that. I'm an introvert too, but I didn't know that I am one for a long part of my life. At that time, I thought that I'm strange, so I just withdrew from any social interactions. Then I gradually opened up because of several life situations, and I got into professional coaching, which helped me as well! Soon after, I stumbled upon the concept of introversion and extraversion. When I started reading more about this topic, I realized that I'm just an introvert...I'm not so weird! :-)

Mimi: Exactly! That was so lovely. Your book took the weirdness out of it. I'm an introvert 100 percent for sure, but it doesn't mean that once in a blue moon I can't be very sociable, you know, and hang out with people, and actually enjoy it! That does happen. But as a rule, it takes energy away from me when I'm with a lot of people. One of my daughters is an extrovert 100 percent of the time. And it energizes her to hang out with people, any kind of people. While with me it has to be a particular kind of person to get me energized.

Gabriela: Same here. It was interesting to discover more about myself and to realize that there are similar people out there! One specific event sparked my interest in helping other introverts: I did a workshop with 40 university students, and at one point I asked how many of them are shy or introverted. Half of them raised their hand! Then I mentioned that I used to be the same, and I worked on myself, and now I'm doing workshops to 40 strangers, leading the group through exercises...and I'm totally okay!

At the end of the workshop, one student reached out to thank me. I'm like: *What did I say? :-)*

"Remember when you asked us to raise our hands? Until that point, I didn't realize that I'm not the only shy person in the world!"

That made me realize that people who are shy or introverted stay so much in their own "bubble" that they might not realize that there are other people like them!

This helped me understand that I want to help these people to connect with others who have the same characteristics so they can understand that they belong to a bigger group (they're not alone), and they can interact with others while still staying true to their nature.

The second thing she mentioned was also interesting: "When you said that you were shy too—but were able to overcome that—you made me realize that I can overcome it too!"

Mimi: That's right! It's really interesting, Gabriela. When I read your book I realized there is so very little information available about introversion. Which is peculiar because most subjects have been discussed to death. But not many people seem to be into this subject. Just yesterday, I was sitting with one of my daughters and her boyfriend and I mentioned that our interview was coming up. And her boyfriend said: "I don't know if I'm an introvert or not." So he had no idea! And I thought: *You're very much an introvert!* I know that because he doesn't want to go to parties. He doesn't like it when I say that we have people coming over: "Will you join us?" He won't. So, you know, he has all the indications of being an introvert and the same with my other daughter. So there are two introverts together: she's very, very shy, my introverted daughter. And so it's wonderful to be able to read research that someone such as you have done, and tips and hints on how to overcome your challenges, and how to bolster your confidence and self-esteem, and participate more. Yeah. So I'm really very appreciative of your work.

Gabriela: Thank you! I'm really curious about how this book with interviews will be received. I think it will be kind of an eye opener for some people, not only to realize they too are introverts but how similar people are using their strengths to overcome challenges—so they become more skillful in overcoming theirs. That's my idea with this book.

Mimi: I thought about it. You see, this is the peculiar thing: we don't necessarily tease it out, we're not trying to figure it out for ourselves. After you said what the book is about, I go: *I don't actually know how I did that because simply I don't think in those terms: introverts, extroverts, techniques or tools I used because that's just me.* You know what I mean?

Gabriela: Yes. That's why I'm doing this as an interview, not just sending you the questions. Because I don't want you to think in terms of extraversion and introversion. This will be part of my comments at the end of the chapter about your challenges: what I take away from your story and what introvert strengths I recognize in the way you handled those situations. You might not be aware of them while we are talking. Let me give you an example. [*I shared a story from another interview for this book.*] Now all you need to do is to focus on your story! :-)

Mimi: It's interesting. I think introverts, often enough, they just help other people to achieve their thing because they work quietly in the background, not so much in the foreground. And that's where I discovered myself. That's what I've done the majority of my life as a wife, as a mother, which by the way, is very common for women. That's what they do. We quietly work in the background to support the people around us. I was always quiet in the background and it has been useful for me with writing.

That's where I feel I can shine because I can quietly write. I like it very much when it's quiet and there's no one there. That's how I can share what I know—a bit of my knowledge —without getting intimidated by people, or sidetracked, or feeling that I need to help them. You see, that's what I feel when I'm out there. I always feel that I'm there to help other people because I'm good at that, I can do that and get joy out of it. But it also uses your life up for the benefit of others. Yet, you're also supposed to get that extra little bit of joy yourself from actually sharing your skills and knowledge that you have acquired over a lifetime. And for me, by doing it in writing, I can reach so many people that I otherwise would never be able to reach.

Gabriela: I like what you said: you like to help. But because of your introversion, you are not socializing too much and helping people…yet you found a way to reach out to more people and help them by sharing what you learned through writing—which is more aligned with your true nature!

Mimi: Yes, very much. If you're more extroverted, then you help people in the office, for instance, or wherever you meet them.

I managed clinics, and there's always a lot of social events connected with that: when people get together—the doctors, nurses—and they have all kinds of discussions. Throughout the year, I've participated in such events, but I find it very hard to go out and socialize. It takes a lot of energy for me to just chit-chat and small talk, and then I come home, and I'm exhausted. So I tried to minimize that, but other people would get pleasure out of it, and then that makes their job very pleasurable and enjoyable. But I get pleasure out of quietly doing what needs to be done. Then often enough you're just subservient to other people, even though you have a lot of knowledge and skills to share. So you need to find a platform to do that, and for me, very much that's in the writing.

Gabriela: Thanks for sharing, Mimi! So, this story was about writing: finding a way to share the information that you wanted to share so you can help more people. Would you like to share another challenge?

Mimi: I've had a lot of challenges in my life, Gabriela. I've dived right in and I had relationship challenges, health challenges, the career challenge I just mentioned...

I think my health challenge was the biggest because I completely crumbled. And with that, everything else around me crumbled: my relationship, my career, my status, the home, everything disappeared. There was really sort of nothing left. That has had the biggest impact on my life. It was like a rebirth pretty much because at various times it looked as if I would die and I didn't. So to me, I'm really living in *Bonus Time* now. So I think: *Well, how can I contribute?* you know? Because this is all my *Bonus Time*, do you know what I mean? It's totally about: what can I contribute now that I wouldn't have been able to had I just disappeared. And that's what my latest book is about: *Live Your Best Life*.

Because I thought that I was going to die for sure, my very last thought when I was in that situation was: *Oh no, what if people go to my home and they open a lingerie drawer, and it's not as tidy as I would like it?*

Then, later on, I beat myself up over that and I thought: *That was my last thought—what if people go and rifle through my stuff?* And I realized that's not good enough, I can live a better life than that. That's just...not good enough!

Then I imagined people at my funeral and what they would say, and I didn't like it. And I go:

No! I can do better than that!

Well, what would you like to do?

I'd like to write and publish books because I had been writing most of my life, but I've never really taken it anywhere. That's what I'm going to do!

And, you know, I said that my *guardian angel* kicked my butt and said: "Well, go out and do something for some people!"

But I was basically lying in bed. You know, the light had been knocked out of me. I wasn't capable of anything. I was lying in bed with the curtains closed, I had earplugs in. I couldn't tolerate light, sound, food, nothing! And yet that thought came back to me:

I have to help some people!

That's ridiculous, I need help!

But the more I thought about it, it made sense: *Well, this is my situation. If I share with people how I overcame it...that would help people!*

That's what started my writing journey. Then my first book, my second, and so on...and I got a lot of satisfaction from that.

That's how I really learned that I work best when I'm left alone. That situation where I was left on my own in a dark room—and this was for years, and years, and years! That was for a long time. But that helped me produce some work and it helped me share my things.

When people come to me, I'm very easy going. I'll go with

the flow. So if people have a lot of stories to tell, I'll just quietly sit there and listen and enjoy them. I don't necessarily feel the need to say: *Oh, but I've got a story too, listen to mine!*

But in the quietness of my room, with people not being able to visit because the viruses and whatever would be bad for me (someone had a cold, for example), I was left to my own devices and that's when I started writing and sharing things.

Gabriela: Wow. This is really powerful! That mind shift that happened when you believed that's your last thought, then realized that you want your life to be different—which started you on a new path, to make the most of your *Bonus Time*, as you coined it!

Such an amazing concept: considering it a *bonus time* and wanting to use it in a more meaningful way: to help people! And that gave you the energy to start writing and find a way to start where you were, using that situation to better yourself and help other people. So powerful!

Mimi: Yes. Very strong. Then I thought: *What do I have to share?*

All I could think is: *I've just been lying in bed for all these years. I'm useless. I'm in the 'too hard basket,' my life is finished. I can't even stand up for more than a few minutes. And my back just collapses on me. I can only just lie in bed.*

It was awful, an awful place to be. And then I thought: *Well I can share, I can actually write about my experiences.* There are many people that have food intolerances. And I could barely tolerate anything. I could tolerate only ten ingredients, and that went on for a long period of five years! That was all I could tolerate for breakfast, lunch, and dinner. And so I thought: *Well, I notice there are a lot of people with food intolerances, allergies, and chemical sensitivities out there.* I thought of these people: they also struggle because for me every single day was a struggle. What to drink? If I drink tap water it would make me sick, so we needed to get a water filter. And if I just ate a slice of bread it would make me sick, and then we had to get gluten-free bread. And even that I couldn't eat for years and years!

Anything that was too dense, like peas, or anything that was too dense…my system just couldn't tolerate! No cheese, no eggs, no meat, none of it! What's left, what can you eat? But I discovered what I could eat. With my girls, together, we found ingredients by trial and error, and eventually, I realized what I can eat. And then we eliminated the everyday drama of what to eat!

But that took a long time. I talk to people now, every day. And someone said: "Oh, I don't know, I've got such a sore gut at night." They don't realize why they have the sore gut. And they don't understand why they have the migraines.

"Well, have you looked at this and that?" I say. "Maybe it's the dairy, maybe it's the gluten, maybe it's the sugar…"

"Oh, it never caused me a problem before!"

"Yeah, but as we age, our body changes. And what didn't use to be a problem, maybe is a problem now."

Then they get back to me: "Wow, my skin cleared up!"

It does make a huge difference to people! And it's absolutely wonderful to be able to do that: through my own pain, and trial, and error, and experimenting, and research…then I can help someone else so easily and say: "Try this, it's easy!"

And it's not that the research isn't out there. I'm not the only person that discovered this; many other people before me have researched it.

But when it's your own personal experience, it seems to be more powerful and really speaks to people! They sit up and they listen. If the doctor says: "Oh, you've got to cut out dairy and gluten and sugar," they go "Yeah, whatever." But then when they talk to me and I tell them my personal story, all of a sudden, they'll take it more seriously. Before they think:

> "That's impossible. What do I live on?"

> "Well, you can live on this because I've done it for years and it works."

It's just beautiful to be able to do that, I absolutely love it!

Gabriela: What I'm taking away from this part of the story is another introvert strength: perseverance. They like to do research, they're curious: *What works for me? Okay, this doesn't work, that doesn't work...* The same way, you kept going and researching and trying different things until you found what works for you. And it worked!

Mimi: It's interesting you say that because I've come across quite a few people who say to me: "I would never have done that. I would just have thrown in the towel."

I could've said: *Okay, that's it. I'm done. I'm out of here. I can't do this, it's too hard.* But to me, it never ever was actually an option because all I could think was: *Yeah, but my kids would be orphans. That can't happen. I can't just leave my kids behind. I need to keep going.*

What is interesting: I wasn't aware that actually there are people that will say, "No, this is too hard. If I can't have my cup of coffee every day, with sugar and milk, I don't want to live."

And I go: "What? For a cup of coffee?" But for some people that is their reality and that's totally fine if you're like that. But I wasn't aware of this because to me you eat to stay alive not the other way around.

Gabriela: You just touched on something else: introverts are motivated from inside. So you found something to motivate you: the idea that your kids will be without you, and you didn't want that to happen! It was something from inside that motivated you to continue, to persevere until you found whatever you needed.

Mimi: Yes.

Gabriela: Do you see how many introvert's strengths are playing in your stories? Did you read the book, *Quiet*, by Susan Cain?

Mimi: No, I don't think I did.

Gabriela: She gathered scientific research about the different characteristics of introverts and extroverts, and wrote the book *Quiet: The Power of Introverts in a World That Can't Stop Talking*. I read it when I was writing my first book. I was looking at what competition would be out there for my book on introverts and job searching. I took a lot of notes about the introvert's characteristics mentioned in her book. And what I did with mine: I considered those characteristics as introverts' strengths, and I showed in my book how they could be used effectively in the context of job hunting. I already had many examples of successful introverted job seekers who used the strategies I was sharing in my book, and I highlighted how using those characteristics helped them succeed. So it's just a matter of leveraging your strengths to overcome your challenges.

Mimi: That makes perfect sense, doesn't it? The way you presented it. What's really interesting: someone else perhaps looked at it and went "Oh, how do I deal with that?" But the moment you call it a strength it becomes a tool you can use from your toolbox, isn't it?

Gabriela: Exactly. And you find ways to use it. If one thing doesn't work for you—because it's not aligned with who you are—you can try another one and another...

Mimi: That's really interesting! You see, my extroverted daughter, for example, she's very outgoing and a very sociable person. When I say to her, "It's so enjoyable to see the ease in how you deal with people," she credits me: "Mom, I only do what I've seen you do!" Which is lovely! The only difference seemingly is that she actually enjoys it and gets pleasure out of it! I do a very similar thing, but I find it taxing! The very similar thing takes energy away from me! This discovery only came to me later in life. I used to feel that I had to go out there, I had to socialize.

That was part of my job and I had to do it, but it took a lot of energy out of me in my early years. I felt that it was expected from me and it was something I had to do. So at the end of the day, I really didn't have anything left—to write or do anything else—because all the energy had been used up spending time with other people.

But as I got older and particularly through my medical emergencies in my illness, I couldn't go out anymore. And that's sort of how I really discovered: *Oh when I'm left to my own devices, I'm very productive.* Partially, probably because all I could do was lie in bed, so there was nothing else I could do other than write, really. So that's what I ended up doing.

But had that not happened, I possibly would never have discovered that as a strength. I always saw it as a weakness because all the people around me were very sociable and they wanted to go out and socialize. And if I found it hard, that was seen as a weakness!

Only when I wasn't able to socialize anymore I discovered—being left to my own devices—that I could use my energy for other things. That was very interesting, I just never looked at it in the light of being an introvert or an extrovert!

Gabriela: I don't think it's very well known. Even if people hear about the concept, they might not get curious to learn more. What you did: you just discovered one of the main characteristics that distinguishes introverts from extroverts: introverts get energy when they are by themselves or in nature. Extroverts get their energy by connecting and talking with people.

That's why your energy was drained when you were talking and socializing, which was taking up all your energy. If you don't take enough time to recharge—you just give, give, give —you get to a point where you start having health problems. I got into a burnout a few years ago because of that. I had a full-time job where I was doing workshops daily and speaking with clients, which drained my energy so much that I couldn't find enough time to recharge…leading to the burnout!

Mimi: That's very true! I noticed that the other day. I've actually just come back from a writing retreat, which is absolutely lovely: it's very quiet, no other people. I still use my industrial-strength earplugs and I put them in. But that's not sufficient because I used to do that for years and what happened—which is funny—as I wore those earplugs, my hearing sharpened! I can still hear the dogs barking. So now I wear industrial-strength mufflers in addition to my earplugs. The other day, a friend took me out and said: "Oh, let's go here and there…" We were in the car, and she has the radio on at the same time she's talking…and my world just falls apart if someone does that! I can't handle it!

Gabriela: Too much noise is overwhelming for an introvert.

Mimi: That's true! Too much noise and I get completely overwhelmed! But for her, this was beautiful. There was all this noise and she was chatting along. And I was sitting there, listening to her and I thought: *Yes indeed, I spent many years like this.* Other people just love the company and the audience they have, but I'm near enough paralyzed because it's all just too much. I need silence! I need quiet. I love, love, love sitting on my veranda! Some butcherbirds come and I share my lunch with them—they sit on my laptop. They just sit there and watch. I love that!

But then other people come and they have that music blaring out from their phones. I just want to crawl in a corner: *Go away, go away!*

"I've got a beautiful song," they say.

"But I already have music," I answer. "Listen, it's nature. Nature is my music and silence is my preferred setting!"

Gabriela: My daughter is also an introvert and when I

listen to her neo-classical compositions for piano it's like a buffer between the external noise and my thoughts! It helps me to stay focused. That's how I was able to write seven to eight hours a day for my first book, while I was recovering from the burnout. Have you tried this kind of music, which allows you to focus?

Mimi: The closest I have come so far is the sound of water-falls. I can concentrate on the sound of waterfalls and then I can filter out all the other noises. Sometimes chimes can do it also: I put the chimes up and that noise can filter other noises. But my preferred setting is always silence, then I'm perfectly happy. And of course, the world isn't like that—it's the opposite!

Gabriela: For extroverts, it's the other way around: they seem to like noises and loud music. But introverts are differ-ent: like you, sitting in your own world. I like to be in my own world too. If I can't, I go to Starbucks, put in my earbuds with my daughter's music, and start writing. This way I don't get disturbed by whatever is around me.

Mimi: It is lovely if you actually can have that music. Our fridge is completely away from my living area. I find it hideous just the noise of the fridge, but not many people seem to feel the same way. I think there are probably more extroverts than introverts. Is that a fair comment or not?

Gabriela: In her book, Susan Cain says that approximately 40 percent of the US population are introverts.

Mimi: I think a lot of your interviewees may well be like me: I have been very much supportive throughout my life—to other people's careers and issues—because that's possibly a role that suits us quietly in the background. Not having to be out there so much and make a noise. But it doesn't mean we don't have skills, talents, and knowledge that would actually contribute in a good way!

Gabriela: That's actually my point: we have a lot to contribute! That's why I'm writing these books for introverts, to help them better understand themselves. We are strategic thinkers, so the world needs us. We are really good leaders if we can get to that level. But in a professional environment that appreciates the extroverted behavior more, it's hard to get to that level.

Yet, if we do—because we think strategically, we do research, we take the time to reflect and go deeper into our reflection —we can come up with better solutions and ideas. Also, we like to connect with people at a deeper level, and that makes meaningful connections. We have many powerful skills. We just need to understand how to use them.

Mimi: Yes, and how to get them out in the world. Because there are so many hoops you have to jump through. Probably some will go: "No, that's just too much. It's taking too much out of me."

Gabriela: Susan Cain presented an interesting concept in her book. She mentioned that introverts could come across as extroverts in specific situations. But if they do it too often— without taking enough breaks—they're at risk of getting burned out. So, from time to time, we can take on that behavior but we have to pay attention to schedule breaks for recharging. Because if we don't, our body gets out of balance and we can even get health problems.

Mimi: This is very good, particularly for younger people, to be aware of it! Because had I been aware of this more, earlier on in my life, I would have lived my life differently. I would have set it up differently. I just wasn't aware of it so much, and I'm very much an introvert. At times, when I'm a little bit energetic, I may actually enjoy just being out with people—even the noise and all the bells and whistles—but only for a limited period of time. Then I need to withdraw. It's not something I will dive in and totally get into because I would just be exhausted from it.

Gabriela: Being introvert doesn't mean that you cannot enjoy being with other people, especially people you connect well with. But we can't do it for a long period of time because our energy dries up very fast. There is scientific proof of why that happens. The pathways in the brain are longer for introverts, they go through the long-term memory first, then to the short-term memory before making a decision. There is much more activity inside an introvert's brain. Plus, they're great observers…noticing a lot of what's happening around them!

So their brain consumes more energy than extroverts', that's why the introverts' energy dries up faster. That's why it is challenging for an introvert to hold on a conversation too long. We can't socialize for too long without feeling drained. Even if we don't get to that point, we still need to withdraw to recharge. Because if we continue that way or the break is not long enough, we won't be able to keep doing what we want. These might seem like little things, but they count!

Mimi: That's so interesting. Particularly when I think of my extroverted daughter: she moves around a lot, very active, she's on social media…we're absolute opposites! She always says to me: "Well, you don't want to socialize." And I go: "No, that's not true! I do want to socialize, but I do it differently. You get dressed and go out, and you stay out for six or eight hours. And you go party, and you drink and listen to loud music. Well, what I would like to do is get dressed and then maybe go to a café and have a cup of tea, and then go back home. And that, maybe for half an hour, an hour max. That's my socializing! If I'm with a couple of friends there, that is lovely! And I'll feel wonderful when I leave. But if you were to make me stay or you take me to a place where there's loud music, then it's a cumbersome punishment!"

Because she only knows socializing the way she does, which is very active—it is dancing, and this and that—she can't even relate to what I do because to her it's not called social! So we're always trying to mix it up because I'm dependent on her for transport. And I go: "You can't just go away for a whole night, have fun and then say: 'Well, mom doesn't like socializing.' Mom does like socializing, but not seven nights a week, not for six hours at a time, and not at the places where you go." It's a completely different concept!

Gabriela: Exactly. Introverts like to socialize too—in their own way—and have a meaningful conversation.

Mimi: That's exactly right! Because this is the other thing: when she goes out and talks about anything and nothing, that's fine. But indeed, I'd like to talk about something in my life that has meaning or is meaningful for that person. Or it makes the world a slightly nicer place for everyone or works toward a project or anything tangible! If it isn't, it just depletes me! And I go: *No, now I'm wasting my Bonus Time. I don't want to be wasting my Bonus Time!*

Gabriela: I love your *Bonus Time* concept!

Mimi: I'm really living that. I feel that acutely, you know, like this is my bonus! Do not waste it, be productive! Not that I have to produce something every day but—energetically—somehow make it better as opposed to leaving it where it is or making it worse.

Gabriela: Great! With this book, I'd like to help introverts understand themselves better and to empower them so they dare to stand up for themselves in front of extroverts. Because sometimes we feel that the extroverts want to impose their own perspective on us, and we don't have the courage to stand up. Or we don't want to, or we don't know how. I feel that, if introverts understand themselves better, they'll get more clarity about how they are and what they can do, and they'll start feeling empowered to do what they want.

Mimi: I'd love to see your work, Gabriela, as part of some school curriculum. At least as part of the discussion. Even if all we can do is make children aware of this. Because if you think about the number of children in schools—and I certainly was one of them—that are labeled "nerd" or "shy" or whatever, and they're just pushed into a corner because they are not the ones that are out there being outrageous, and crazy, and busy.

They are actually quietly studying and doing their thing. And instead of people saying: "Oh, well done, good job!" They go: "Oh, why don't you just get out there, do more sport, do more this, do more that..." It's just not our strength! But it's not recognized. And because this isn't recognized, it kind of sets you up for a whole life of, you know, what you do isn't as worthy as what someone else does! It'll be lovely to be able to create some kind of shift in society. And I think your work is certainly pushing toward that, and I applaud you for that! I think it's wonderful! I really do.

Gabriela: Thank you so much, Mimi! Actually, you're not the first person who's telling me to go and help teenagers or young adults. These ideas came from some workshops that I've done before, which I put in my books (the photo-coaching book series, for example). Some people told me: "This could be very good for teenagers. They are at a place where they need to understand these concepts." And what you're saying makes me think that I should create a photo-coaching book for introverts.

Mimi: Yeah, I think you should. I'm just throwing the idea out there, you do whatever you want. But you know, sometimes children's books are only like 12 or 20 pages long. If there were to be a book about two friends: one is an introvert, the other an extrovert (no one knows this of course), then the extrovert gets all the applause and all the attention. I'll see the introvert quietly plows away without much recognition. Then somewhere in the book, they'll be able to come up with: "Ah, you're an introvert!" and: "Ah, you're an extrovert!…and that it's equally valued! Because very often they aren't equally valued in society.

Even if you look, for instance, in the movie industry. There are people in society who do very good work. Erin Brockovich, for instance. An American legal clerk and environmental activist who was instrumental in building a case against the Pacific Gas and Electric Company of California in 1993. She did an enormous amount of research to find out that the government was doing a dodgy on these people, and she brought it out in the open. Then someone made a movie about this, and who gets all the praise and all the money? It's the extras, and actresses, the actors, but not the person that actually, quietly, has been plowing away, doing the research, doing all the hard work! She doesn't get much. Yes, her name was mentioned.

That's just society, isn't it? We need our idols and we go: "Wow, these people are so wonderful!" But no, they're not at all, they're just actors who are faking it and are getting paid money to do so. The real heroes are the people who actually did the work, their stories, those are the real heroes! And if we had any sense whatsoever, we would give all that money —that actors now get—we would give it to them so they can continue to do that good work!

Gabriela: I totally understand and agree with you! I had in mind to start doing workshops based on my photo-coaching books. I noticed in Susan Cain's book a characteristic for introverts (not only in me): we can be at extremes, either quiet by ourselves (doing our own work) or in a leadership role. But not somewhere in between. I'm not comfortable to be part of a group. It took me time to discover that because when I was just quiet, shy, I could never imagine that I can be a leader. But when I started working on myself through coaching, that's what came out from it—that I'm a leader!

Then, when I start taking on leadership roles, I realized that I have to pay attention to my energy, to not overdo it. Now I'm writing books, I'm putting them out there, but something is missing. I miss the other parts (workshops, leadership).

So recently, I started the Immigrant Writers Association. I really want to empower other introverts in general, and many writers are introverts. And I want to empower immigrants like me. Because we come from other countries, we already overcame some challenges, and starting from scratch again is a struggle: transitioning to a world where no one knows you, getting yourself up-to-date. Yet, you have a lot to contribute, a lot to offer to the world! With other 12 immigrants, we incorporated the association and we started programs to help immigrants write and publish books.

Mimi: Wow. Where are you from originally?

Gabriela: Romania. I'm in Canada now.

Mimi: Canada. So that would be tough, wouldn't it?

Gabriela: I wouldn't say so. And if we talk about introverts, I guess my introverted side helped me. I didn't socialize and try to do things that are not true to my introverted nature. Introverts like to see the big picture, for example. So when I came to Toronto, I went to the top of the CN Tower on the fourth day, to get a sense of where I was (I couldn't get it from the street level). I always look at the bigger picture first, then I figure out what I can do, and how I can use my strengths. It played very well for me: I changed careers from engineering to coaching (three years after I came here), so I carved my career path in a totally different direction. Now I'm doing the same with writing. I guess the inner strengths of an introvert play a lot when you need to go through challenges. That helped me, for sure!

Mimi: Wow. Wow. Wow. That's just amazing!

The other thing that came to me when you say teenagers: I think that's a perfect time to talk to them because this is the time when they're looking for their identity, and they go: "Who am I?"

I look at my girls, 28 years old and 31. I mentioned your books to them several times—especially to my introverted daughter (she's very, very shy). But at her age, she's not that interested. They've sort of established who they think they are and they're just doing it.

At my age, you become interested again and you go: "Well, why did this happen? And how?"

I'm reflecting and trying to adjust course. But she's not there, she's actually solidly now setting it. So that wouldn't work. This is just personal experience looking at her. I think teenage or even primary school-age, that would be the time to grab them and say: "Hey listen..."

Just listening to you Gabriela, just a few things that you throw out like: "We see the larger picture." I've always been the one wherever I am, I'm always seeing the larger picture. And you say: "We are not seen to be leaders," but actually, when my daughter goes out, I'm the one who sits quietly in the background for like a half an hour and I'll put a whole itinerary together for my daughter: "you go here, you do this and that..." She doesn't. She just bursts out into the world and does stuff. And I plan it out: "if you could do this then you can fit that and there's still money to do this and that..." But she doesn't because her brain just doesn't do that kind of stuff, you know? Not even with the time, let alone with the money and how to fit it all in. But I can do that meticulously, effortlessly, it means nothing to me. It's just time, and I just do that. And only talking to you do I understand that those kinds of skills are part of being an introvert. This is really nice. It becomes something to celebrate, really!

Gabriela: Exactly!

Mimi: It's really nice, and I just never realized! You see, people sit down and nitpick about bits, and they keep talking about tiny things...and I go: "But it's all irrelevant. It's about the large picture. It doesn't matter. These are tiny minor details, you know, we don't have to spend time on them. It'll fall into place."

And then I'm the person again that's on the outside because everyone is so involved with all the finer details. And I go: "No, no, no, they come later! We want to have the big picture first."

Gabriela: Interesting. I'm thinking: this discussion could become a book in itself.

Mimi: It's really, really interesting. I really like it! It's great because it's opening my mind, and all of a sudden, I'm understanding things I didn't use to before...things and situations are being demystified. I was wondering why people didn't appreciate me?

Gabriela: I have another story, about my first photo-coaching book (*Meeting With My Self: Self-Coaching Questions That Invite Wisdom In*). I released it initially as a deck of cards a few years ago, and I gave one to a coaching client. After the coaching relationship ended, we didn't stay in touch for a while. But when I published my second photo-coaching book (*Navigating the Relationship Landscape: Practical Guide*), she reached out to me with a question and then we caught up with what happened since we last talked. She's divorced now but she went through a tough situation with her teenage daughter, who didn't speak for a while. She closed herself so much—and didn't want to speak—that 48 therapy and psychology sessions didn't help her!

One day, she found the photo-coaching cards that I gave to her mom earlier, and she went through them one by one. The day she finished answering the coaching questions from those cards, she opened up to her mom for the first time telling her what happened: her dad tried to kill her! She gave more details to her mom. I can only imagine how traumatic that event was for her! She's still going through some of those cards daily and told her mom: "This set of photo-coaching questions is exactly what teenagers need! They don't need to be told what to do. They need these kinds of cards that ask them questions so they can figure it out by themselves. Every therapist who works with teenagers should have these cards!"

I was like: "Wow, this is huge!" I'm happy that I learned how to self-publish books because I was able to publish that set of photo-coaching cards as a book on Amazon so more people have access to it. That's why I'm thinking to start working with teenagers. I just have to figure out how to reach out to them.

Mimi: That sounds fabulous, what your cards achieved! I did something similar with my last book, *Live Your Best Life*. I asked people: "What would you want people to say about you at your funeral?" It stops them in their tracks, and they go: "Oh!" Then the magic seems to happen! Once they start saying "This is what I would like them to say..." and you ask "Is your lifestyle that way?" they realize they can adjust their lifestyle slightly…and all of a sudden, they're in control!

Whereas prior to that, life just happens to you, kind of thing, doesn't it?

The funny thing with me, as soon as I decided what I'd like to do (I want to be an author) within one, two years I've written and published five books, and they're all bestsellers. That's amazing! And that was just a mind shift from think-ing: *No, I don't want people talking about me like that.* In my imagi-nation they were saying bad things, then I thought: *No, I'm capable of more. I can contribute more!* I'm actually doing it, and it manifested quite effortlessly. It wasn't like people say: "You have to do goal setting and this and that..." it goes much, much easier and smoother than that!

Gabriela: I had a similar experience to share about my first photo-coaching book. In one chapter, there is an image with a cross and the questions: "What would you like to achieve in this life? Are you taking daily steps to get there?"

A client who went through that book had a huge *"AHA!"* when she saw that page. She was thinking of suicide prior to looking at this book, but that image really spoke to her. She realized that just because she had a very difficult life so far, it doesn't have to be the same the rest of her life. She put the suicidal thoughts aside, went back to school, and started a new career.

Mimi: Isn't that amazing?

Gabriela: It is!

Mimi: It's interesting how little things and stuff can get in the way. Another example: I'm sharing the house with my daughters, which is lovely, and I'm happy about it. But there are little things, like the kettle, for instance. They're using it, and when all the water is gone I have to fill it. So I decided to get my own kettle. So for 20 bucks, all of a sudden I've got my own kettle and there'll always be water in it!

So it's little bits and pieces like that which you can adjust in your life, and it makes all the difference to your enjoyment or how you live your life. As opposed to just chugging along and not necessarily being happy or finding it a struggle, or hard.

You can look at it from a different perspective, thinking:

how can you eliminate stresses and make it a bit more enjoyable for yourself as well as for others? Because of course now there's no more nagging, you know? The main thing was actually that one of my daughters uses unfiltered water, but I can't drink unfiltered water. That means, after she uses it, it needs to be emptied and I have to put in filtered water. And that was a major drama, which you don't need every day. And it was as simple as buying a separate kettle.

So sometimes life seems hard. But you can look at it and go: *No, actually it doesn't have to be.* You can make it easy quite quickly.

Gabriela: Yes, but you have to think about it and what you can do.

Mimi: That's exactly right. It doesn't happen automatically. You have to take some kind of action. And have a shift of awareness.

Gabriela: Yes, you have to distance yourself first. Then the awareness is there, you just need to pay attention to it and go: *Oh, I can do this!*

Mimi: That's right. I do find Gabriela—and I don't have answers for this—but if you want to be very big in your field and do a lot, it does involve a certain amount of socializing. Going out there, talking to people, and I simply do not have the energy for that. So I'm very happy to be at the grassroots level and just put out the information and trust that the universe will guide the proper people there.

Because socializing, getting out there, and putting your name out constantly requires a lot of energy. I look at my daughter: she has that bubbly energy and she can sustain it. Right now,

I can either write a book or I can promote it, but I can't do both.

But knowing that this is part of me being an introvert, all of a sudden gives me a place to be. And it'll make it easier for me to stand my ground, as opposed to saying: *Well, the world is full of extroverts and if you don't fit in then…* You know what I mean.

Even me at my age, knowing now that I'm an introvert is giving me that extra little confidence and extra little identity which has been lacking all my life. And all of a sudden my talents are appreciated, you know? In my head, they're good things, as opposed to *Oh, something I should be slightly embarrassed about because it's not the norm.*

Gabriela: Wow, that is powerful!

Mimi: Yes! It's really very powerful because it affected my life in many different ways. And I think a lot of introverts, we may be just gentle, quiet souls, quietly plowing away, and not really getting the recognition because our world is a loud world. Whoever's the loudest, making the most noise out there, they are the people that get the attention.

Gabriela: From what I remember from Susan Cain's book, it doesn't seem that it's like that all over the world.

Chinese culture coined the term "quiet leadership." I love it! The Japanese, Chinese, and Norwegian cultures appreciate more the introverted characteristics. I look at extroverts and introverts being like *Yin* and *Yang*, they complement each other's strengths. That's why we have both extroverts and introverts in the world. And look, there are whole countries that appreciate more introversion than extroversion, while in other parts of the world it's the other way around.

So it looks like this *Yin* and *Yang* concept applies to the world at large (some countries appreciate something while others appreciate the opposite). While for projects, if you know how to nurture both introverted and extroverted personalities, they'll work better together and achieve more. So it's a very interesting concept to explore at another level.

Mimi: That is interesting actually, I hadn't thought about it. Because of course we look at the world from our own cultural backgrounds and we think the whole world is like that, which of course it isn't. So that is a really interesting point. It's very much the Western world, isn't it? Where we value people that are a bit louder. That's how I see it. How would you say that? It's not fair, to say that they're a bit louder.

Gabriela: They appreciate more the extroverted behavior. Here's something I found interesting: a former HR manager left a review for the first book I published (*Introverts: Leverage Your Strengths for an Effective Job Search*). She mentioned that it was normal for her to hire extroverts because they were able to articulate their strengths and talk with confidence about what they did. They opened up showing who they are so she could better understand who she's hiring. But introverts didn't. She couldn't get much about how they are since they didn't talk much about themselves. And introverts don't like to talk about themselves! It's not that they are not good, they are just not so comfortable talking about themselves—even if they know they're good.

Mimi: Yeah, it's not something we think needs to be advertised, sort of.

Gabriela: So from an HR perspective, it's interesting to see why extroverted people get jobs more easily—because they open up! And introverted people don't because they don't open up enough! That's why my book is focusing more on how you can find a job by going where there is less or no competition (the hidden market), and how you can meet the employer midway in an interview. Because there are ways you can project the real image of who you are and what you have to offer, even if you stay true to your introverted nature. You can make them interested in you when you play to your strengths in a discussion at an equal level: *I need you, you need me.* So I kind of turned around the whole concept of job searching in that book, for those who have the patience to go through it.

Mimi: Yes, it's great, all the different angles you looked at. You're really opening my mind, which I like. And it can help you in everything that you do in life if you can have that perspective.

Gabriela: Yes. When something is not working, just look at it from another perspective!

Mimi: That's exactly right! Just a little bit of extra awareness can make all the difference. And you know, Gabriela, a lot of us are just sort of in a rut. We've been conditioned by our parents, by our cultural background, and we take all that for normal. We can't even see the other possibilities, we're just not aware of them.

Gabriela: We're not even told there are other possibilities.

Mimi: Hmm, so you think they don't even exist today if you've never seen or heard about them.

Gabriela: They exist, you just don't see them.

Mimi: No, you can't see them. That's right! So here in your books, you are showing them how to re-phrase and re-label. You're definitely opening up my mind, and I really like it. And I would definitely want to see what you do as part of a curriculum in some way. It will make a huge difference to a lot of people—to 40 percent of the population, which is a lot!

Gabriela: I think it would be more than 40 percent because even extroverts could benefit if we open their eyes about how introverts are.

Mimi: You're right. And I wasn't so much aware, even after I read your book (but I probably forgot), you said that our brains work differently. And that makes perfect sense to me! I think we're capable of longer conversations about something tangible, but way less conversation about the weather and things like that. And that you don't find many introverts because they don't go out. So you tend to bump into extroverts.

Gabriela: Exactly! And you say: *Oh, the world is full of extroverts!* No! It's because introverts don't go out much. One of the problems I have: I was going to put this in a curriculum and create workshops for companies, but I have to put info about both extroverts and introverts because they might say: "We're not interested, because we have both. Why would you come in and have us pay you to talk about only half of them?"

Mimi: Ok, that makes sense. So how are you going to deal with that?

Gabriela: While I was writing the book for introverts and job searching, I had a mentor (an extrovert) who was pushing me to go to companies to build my coaching business. So I

designed a workshop on the different characteristics of extroverts and introverts, and how they can be leveraged to
improve the team's productivity. Then we had a similar
discussion—like the one I'm having with you now—since she
wanted to give me feedback on how I designed that workshop. And her reaction was exactly like yours: "Oh, you
opened my eyes! Now I understand why that lady was
behaving that way yesterday, which was quite frustrating!"

Mimi: Well, I think it's different for people at different
periods of life. I can see that for both of my daughters, it
doesn't do much for them. They listen, and they go like:
"introverts, extroverts...yeah, yeah, yeah..." And then just
move on with their life, without making any adjustments.
They don't actually gain the extra awareness. They're just
quite set. But I think for teenagers it'll be brilliant; even in
primary school, I would think. And people my age too,
because you look back over your life and you go: *Oh wow,
oh wow!*

I think most of us at this age do reflect on our lives because
what we've done the first 30 years was just being silly, I guess.
Then the next 30 years is hard work. And now you know, if
you're lucky enough to get another 30 years, you're reflecting
and thinking: *Well, how can I improve? Can I do better?* And what
you're giving us, to me anyway, you're giving me some tools
that will make it easier. And the tools were there all along,
but I didn't realize because it was just a matter of re-labeling,
really. That is very useful! I think not all people, of course,
but certainly a substantial group of people will go: "Hmm,
what am I going to do with the rest of my life?" You know?
And it's nice to have those extra tools available. Thank you!

Gabriela: You're welcome, Mimi!

I'm really curious to learn what you got from this interview (and from the next ones). After all, what's most important is the impact that a book has on us, both short and long-term. Because you would like to get something out of the time and energy spent reading a book, wouldn't you?

Now let's talk about the *introvert strengths* that I've noticed throughout the conversation I had with Mimi. The longer we spoke, the more her strengths came to the surface.

√ Introverts get along well with other introverts

Since introverts share the same personality traits, they understand each other quite well. As you probably noticed, that's what happened with Mimi and me. Although it was the first time we talked in real life, we covered many topics and were able to carry on the conversation for almost two hours (we thought that it'd be about 40 minutes). Until this interview, we just exchanged a few Facebook messages related to writing or self-publishing.

√ Introverts are open to sharing information about themselves in one-on-one conversations and an environment they feel comfortable with

Despite what we often hear, introverts do open up in certain situations. And one-on-one conversations suit them well. I'm pretty sure that neither Mimi nor I would share so much about ourselves if it wasn't a one-on-one conversation. What helped even more was the interview format: it was online, using the Zoom.us platform, having headsets, which allowed us to focus on the conversation, without getting distracted or overwhelmed by the outside noise or things happening around us.

Mimi's interview, her books, and all the other stories shared in the following chapters are a living proof that introverts open up when they're comfortable or have a meaningful purpose in mind.

✓ When they resonate with something, introverts reflect on how it applies to and affects their own life

While reading my first book, Mimi realized that she's a *100 percent introvert*, which completely changed the way she looked at and understood the different situations and challenges of her own life. Through self-reflection, she realized that it was like removing a veil that had been in front of her eyes for all those years, without realizing. It gave her a framework to understand herself better.

✓ Introverts instinctively isolate themselves often from the outside world

Often seen as a weakness by some people, I consider this a strength because it allows introverts to withdraw and recharge, and come back to the world regenerated, ready to contribute in one way or another.

Yet, taken to an extreme, too much isolation will serve neither the introvert nor others. Introverts also feel the need to connect, and too much isolation affects them—with or without realizing why!

Mimi felt the need to withdraw from social interactions even early in her life. But without understanding the positive aspect of this need, she considered it *weird* and forced herself to comply with what she thought was the *norm* (according to society's rules).

✓ Introverts get motivated by meaningful causes, bigger than themselves

Introverts crave meaningful connections—meaningful to them, to others—and to make the world a slightly nicer place.

Mimi's willingness to help others gave her the energy and motivation to reinvent her life (making the most of her *Bonus Time*), even if her health was in a very precarious situation (bedridden for years, weak body, intolerance to food and light).

✓ Introverts are strategic thinkers

After realizing what she doesn't want (the *final* thought that *woke her up*), she figured out what she wants: to write books and help others. And from there, she starts looking into what she already has (knowledge and time), and what else she needs, and starts taking steps to become the inspiring best-selling author that she is now, a few years later.

✓ Introverts are not afraid to become trailblazers, committed to helping others and increase their awareness

Being driven by meaningful causes, they are willing to push a shift in society.

After overcoming her own struggles, Mimi is now helping others, not only through her inspiring survival story, but also with what she learned in the process. Through her *Bonus Time* concept and insightful advice (gained through research and personal experience), she became a trailblazer in her immediate community and worldwide (through her books and counseling).

✓ Introverts don't seek recognition. They are happy to focus in the background on meaningful objectives

Mimi gave several examples, including an introvert's research that was featured in a movie. Erin Brockovich put a lot of time and energy in the research that was featured in the movie, not for recognition but because she was driven by a meaningful cause.

✓ Introverts do well in environments that support and nurture their personality

As Mimi discovered, left on her own in a quiet environment or nature, she was quite productive and enjoyed what she was doing (writing).

Examples of environments that suit well the introverts: a quiet environment (allows them to focus), nature (soothing, regenerating, recharging), classical music or white noise (helps to concentrate, masking distracting sounds).

✓ Introverts are great observers of both the inner and outer worlds

This comes naturally to introverts.

Without being so conscious about her inner world, Mimi couldn't have discovered her *Bonus Time*, the thought that came back several times (*she wants to help others*)—while she was dealing with her difficult health condition. Also, it helped her to find the motivation and courage to fight for her life and help others (those who go through similar struggles, her daughters, etc.).

Mimi felt overwhelmed when her friend talked and listened to loud music simultaneously. That's because introverts are very aware and pick up signs from both their inner and outer worlds, which could easily lead to stress and being over-whelmed.

Yet, this is also a strength: such acute awareness—if caught before it becomes overwhelming—can provide great insights, understanding of others' behavior and struggles, and prevent situations from getting worse.

√ Introverts love to help others

It's part of their being! They're always ready to help, which makes them great friends, colleagues, partners, teachers…

But as Mimi mentioned, taken to an extreme—always thinking of and helping others—this could leave them depleted of energy and without much time to express them-selves, what they think or believe in, or focus on what they'd like to do.

√ Introverts are social beings

Although we often hear otherwise, introverts do feel the need to connect and socialize sometimes. Yet, as Mimi recognized, the introvert's way of socializing is totally different than the extrovert's. Becoming aware of the differences and staying true to your nature is what could make socializing more enjoyable for introverts.

√ Introverts are good at expressing themselves and communicate in non-verbal ways

Verbal communication is not the only way for self-expression and communicate your thoughts and ideas.

While introverts could become great at verbal communication if they want to, it's more natural to them to use other ways of communication. Mimi found that writing suits her well.

Finding the way that suits you best and uses your strengths will allow you to share your knowledge and wisdom—and even communicate—without completely isolating yourself from others.

✓ Being curious is a strength; making introverts ask thoughtful questions and build genuine connections (even with extroverts)

Mimi's question after discovering her *Bonus Time: "Well, how can I contribute?"* led her to find a way to help others, which shifted her life toward a more meaningful direction.

She also mentioned several times the genuine connections she's been able to make while communicating with others.

✓ Introverts don't rely only on one way of learning

There are several learning styles; visual, kinesthetic, and auditory…to name a few! Check out the Multiple Intelligence Theory to learn more and become aware of your style. Verbal communication is not the only way to get information and insights.

Visualizing herself at her funeral—imagining what people would say—gave Mimi new insights to consider, which turned her life around.

✓ Introverts are great thinkers

Introverts spend a lot of time focusing inward. So pondering different ideas and concepts, and analyzing and synthesizing data comes naturally to them. They can deal with abstract concepts, make connections between various experiences and fields; and extrapolate the information to a new level of understanding.

Did you notice Mimi's ability to take learning about the introvert's strengths to a broader perspective, beyond her personal life? For example, she thought about how different age groups (children, teenagers, adults, and older adults) can be affected, and the impact on their life if they become more aware of the introvert's strengths.

✓ Introverts are creative

And creativity is not limited to art! Mimi became creative with what she can do with her *Bonus Time.*

Thinking of how children could be exposed to the introvert's and extrovert's strengths, Mimi suddenly got an idea for a children's book, and all the struggles children could be spared throughout their life if they learn about these strengths at an early stage.

✓ Introverts are capable of sustained research

Mimi proved this ability by tirelessly researching information for several years (while she was bedridden) on what could improve her health condition. Through trial and error, and compiling the data gathered, she was finally able to find the ten ingredients that helped her to stay alive and recover.

✓ Introverts are perseverant and have a sense of duty

The above example also shows Mimi's capacity to persevere, especially since she found a meaningful objective for her—to continue to be part of her daughters' lives!

Since introverts are motivated from inside, finding the right reason, which is meaningful to you, will activate this strength: *perseverance*.

✓ Introverts are capable of identifying the bigger picture

At one point, Mimi mentioned her frustration that others spend time in identifying details, thus missing the most important part: the bigger picture.

Once you understand the broader context, focusing on the details will become more productive and efficient.

✓ Introverts like collaboration while extroverts like competition

Even for small things, introverts don't like to *fight* for what they need. That's why Mimi looked into a solution that eliminated the conflict and competition over the kettle, by buying her own. No more friction with her daughters if there's water in the kettle or not. :-)

✓ Introverts are out-of-the-box thinkers

I love how Mimi pointed out my *way of looking* at introverts' characteristics as strengths, calling it *re-framing and re-labelling*! Looking from this fresh perspective, the same characteristics become strengths, which can be used as *tools* in the *introvert's toolbox* for overcoming challenging situations and moving forward. A fresh way of looking at introverts' characteristics, isn't it?

If you didn't know, here's a small list of famous introverts who are out-of-the-box thinkers:

• Albert Einstein (mathematician, physicist, developed the theory of relativity, won Nobel Prize)
• Isaac Newton (mathematician, physicist, astronomer, theologian, author)
• Abraham Lincoln (lawyer, politician, 16th US president)
• Mahatma Gandhi (lawyer, politician, social activist, writer, leader of the Indian independence movement against British rule)
• Charles Darwin (naturalist, developed the theory of evolution by natural selection)
• Nikola Tesla (inventor, electrical engineer, mechanical engineer, futurist)
• Bill Gates (business magnate, founder of Microsoft, investor, author, philanthropist, humanitarian)
• Larry Page (computer scientist, Internet entrepreneur, co-founder & CEO of Google)
• Steve Wozniak (co-founder of Apple, inventor, electronics engineer, programmer, philanthropist, technology entrepreneur)
• Elon Musk (founder, CEO & Product Architect of Tesla Motors, technology entrepreneur, investor, engineer)
• Mark Zuckerberg (co-founder & CEO of Facebook, technology entrepreneur, philanthropist)

Isn't it interesting? We often hear that we should focus on only one thing but all these introverts became famous because they've used their strengths and combined knowledge from several fields!

√ Once introverts know what they want, the journey becomes more enjoyable

As Mimi mentioned, when she realized what she wanted (to

write books), and allowed herself to *walk that path*, it became easier and even enjoyable to write books for nine years.

————————

I could find more introvert strengths in Mimi's interview, but I thought that you might be eager to read the next chapter.

————————

List of Introverts' Strengths
covered in this book
gabrielacasineanu.com/list-introverts-strengths

Chapter Two

ALEX

I would look at them and sometimes I would say: "This is not true! I'm not going to say that because I've already done my research and I know ..."

— ALEX RASCANU

If you caught yourself thinking, while reading the previous chapter, that you're not at Mimi's age yet, I invite you to meet Alex now. He's much younger (probably around Mimi's daughters' age) and has been aware of his introversion since his teenage years.

At the beginning of Mimi's interview, I shared with her one of the Alex's stories. I noticed in myself and while talking to other introverts (some interviewed in this book) that we have so many thoughts and ideas going on in our minds that sometimes we need a starting point to catalyze those thoughts and ideas into what we need.

As you'll see from Alex's interview, he was able to do this before our meeting. As an analytical introvert, he made sure he understood what I'm asking, prepared his *homework*, and presented it in 30 minutes (the duration of his break).

How did I come to know Alex? Someone introduced us when Alex was looking for a few more people to interview for his first book: *How to Reach Your Potential*. Since I was looking for introverted interviewees—and he looked like one—I asked if he'd be interested in being interviewed for my book project! :-)

He was a program coordinator in the non-profit sector and was about to move to Nova Scotia to pursue a Master in Public Administration at Dalhousie University. So I caught him just in time. :-)

Gabriela: Alex, please tell us about one of your challenges and how you were able to overcome it.

Alex: The first big challenge that I faced in my life was when we moved to Canada from Romania when I was 16 years old. I moved here with my parents and my brother, and I couldn't speak English. That was a big challenge! As an introvert, I already had some difficulties connecting with others. I was also quite analytical, and I had played chess professionally in Romania for many years. I was not the kind of person that really went out much. Coming here and not speaking the language is quite difficult!

What I ended up doing: I went into my *comfort zone* and joined the chess club at school. I was able to make quite a few friends that way! One of my closest friends took me to the boxing club where he was training, for example. This way— step by step—I became more comfortable speaking in

English. I think I had the vocabulary from reading and watching movies, but I couldn't speak the language. So genuinely connecting with others in the space that I felt comfortable in, proved to be a really good thing—it really helped me!

So perhaps a lesson for me from that challenge is: go to your comfort zone where you know that you're good at or you like to do and—in that environment—you can connect with people. That way you're not at a level below them, you're playing in the same space. It's an enjoyable experience for everyone, and you can grow in that environment. That helped me tremendously!

Another big challenge that I faced was when I started a new job after graduating from the University of Toronto. I did a business degree and specialized in public administration because I fell in love with the teaching style of one professor —he was teaching public management. I was also reading about politics and public administration because when we were in Romania, my grandfather was actually involved in the revolution. He was imprisoned; he was part of this secret party that was fighting for the end of communism. So I had this interest in political activism. It hadn't really manifested in a larger way beyond just being involved in student government and university governance—it wasn't out in the real world!

After graduation, I applied and ended up having the opportunity to work for a member of parliament. I initially joined as a special assistant, but within two weeks of having that role, the legislative assistant (who does old House of Commons work) quit because he wanted to pursue a master's degree. When I was given the opportunity, I became a legislative assistant, dealing with old House of Commons speech writing, media relations, and drafting bills. A very significant portfolio for a 22-year-old! Almost everyone in that role was 35 plus, same as the other members of parliament.

The way I think I learned was to blend in and really try to perform well on the job—even though it was very new to me. It was extremely challenging to be in that very fast paced environment where you could be getting 100 to 200 phone calls and emails you had to answer every day, with a lot of different types of requests.

One day, two individuals were decapitated in some region and there was a political issue. Then that was raised to the international level in terms of media coverage. And those individuals happened to be in a group that has some sort of relationship with the control group of the member of parliament that I was working for. Therefore, he had to make a statement about it because we were getting phone calls and emails on the issue, plus the media was calling wanting to see what he thinks about it and if there's anything that we can do. So we ended up the very same day writing letters to the prime minister of a country, to other top senior politicians in different parts of the world, drafting media releases and doing all kinds of things, you know. And that was a normal day. It was just phenomenal! Every day there was something else.

Another day you get a thousand petitions about an issue, 750 on one side and 250 are the exact opposite, and you have to answer all of them. And how do you answer in a way that—in my mind—is truthful? You know, being careful with your language while at the same time working on the issue that's at hand.

For me, given my personality, an introvert, more analytical than perhaps other people, I would say that I tried to gather as much information as possible before I made any statement to anyone. I made sure I was reading the Globe & Mail, National Post, and Toronto Star every morning. Reading online as well. And when I was getting talking points from the party's leadership about what we should say on an issue, I would look at them and sometimes I would say: "This is not true! I'm not going to say that because I've already done my research and I know what the truth is." And therefore, I was able to be more careful and not necessarily follow what I was being told. I was able to actually articulate a point that was truthful on the issue while, at the same time, trying to ensure that we don't cause an additional thousand emails in regards to the issue.

What I learned in that role is that preparation is really, really important! Someone like myself, who has an analytical nature, can perform really well by using that strength. And we can deliver quality results and communications material, and whatever else we're working on because we actually take the time to do the necessary research before we launch a new initiative. I think that leadership is not necessarily starting something blindly, just launching it without proper background research, just because you have enough charisma to do whatever you want. I think that you have to be aware of the social and economic issues that are involved in the project that you're working on. And have that in mind as you're developing your initiative or working on it.

Another challenge I had: to stay within a specific workplace environment. I was working in a market research role for one of the largest chocolate manufacturers—which may not be surprising given the kind of person that I am. I was able to do that role well for a couple of years. But then it became challenging to stay in it. Because I started to learn not just how to sell more of the product, and how to develop new products that more individuals will buy and consume, but I also started to learn more about who the user is. And the fact that the individuals that were most predisposed to using that particular product (chocolate), were actually the type of individuals who should have less of it!

I was looking at research reports where individuals who were on welfare, who didn't have money and were borrowing money to buy chocolate so that they can feel better about their situation because they needed something! And that was just one scenario. But there were so many other similar scenarios, so over time, I didn't feel as comfortable being in that role! Maybe someone else would but not me. Because I didn't just look at the numbers, I was looking at the emotional aspect of what kind of impact this job actually has. By digging that out, it really connected with me and I said: "I'm not doing this anymore. I'm going to change to doing something else." That's where I can go to sleep at night and I can feel happy that I'm doing something meaningful in the world.

Gabriela: That's powerful. Thanks for sharing!

Throughout the interview with Alex, I noticed many of the *introvert strengths* highlighted in the previous chapter. Here are some more with examples from Alex's stories:

√ Introverts are perfectionists

Being a perfectionist could be a strength (*thrive for excellence*) and a weakness (*if you get stuck into "it's not enough"*).

Alex's perfectionism helped him to understand that not speaking English was a weakness, but that motivated him to do something about it, instead of allowing it to decrease his self-esteem!

His willingness to thrive for perfection helped him perform well on all the jobs he's had so far, no matter how challenging they were.

✓ Aware of their inner world, introverts understand that the "comfort zone" comprises different *sub-zones*

We could be quite comfortable in some of our *sub-zones*, and little or not at all in others.

While Alex was not comfortable living in an English environment without being able to speak the language—let's call it his *English sub-zone*—he was aware of his strength in the *Playing Chess sub-zone*.

✓ Understanding the power of verbal communication, introverts can find a genuine way to improve theirs

Alex relied on what he was good at—the *Playing Chess sub-zone* —and used that to find an environment that allowed him to reach his objectives: improve his spoken English, meet people, and make friends in the new country.

✓ Introverts do well in a situation where they feel at the same level

That's why Alex chose to join the chess club at school. He felt at the same level in that environment, where he could rely on his non-verbal communication (specific to the chess game).

✓ Spending time focusing inwardly helps introverts become more aware of their strengths

Alex is very aware of his analytical skills and considers them his strength. He was able to make the most of it by choosing professional environments and positions that greatly benefit from this strength.

✓ Introverts pay attention to what they resonate with

Alex deeply resonated with his grandfather's involvement in a political cause. Instead of ignoring this aspect and the social impact it can have on a larger scale, Alex carves his professional path driven by what deeply resonates with him: fresh out of university he chose to work for the parliament, then in the non-profit sector, now pursuing his master's degree in public administration.

✓ Introverts are good at tackling complex problems

The examples Alex gave related to his work at parliament speak for themselves. And his analytical mind helped him deal effectively with those problems, even if they seemed scary at the beginning.

✓ Introverts are quite mature for their age

Due to their inward focus, introverts are deep thinkers. They easily tap into their intuition, and self-reflection is a usual practice for them.

Alex's performance in the position at the parliament— usually held by more senior professionals—proved his ability.

✓ Introverts are courageous when motivated by passion

Alex's ability to take on a very challenging role (his first job), then switching fields and sectors with ease, shows his courage and willingness to take on challenges that others might not. All of this is led by his passion for making an impact on a larger scale.

✓ Integrity and values are important to introverts

Alex stood up and defended his point of view in front of parliament leaders when his research revealed important aspects regarding the issues at stake.

He also quit his comfortable position in the marketing department of the chocolate company when he realized the impact of his work had the opposite effect of helping people (what he desired).

Honesty is one of the most important values for many introverts.

✓ Introverts are great researchers

Several examples showed Alex's research skills. I'll also mention these skills are not only work-related or focused on the outside world. Knowing the topic of this interview, Alex was able to *dig* inside and be well prepared for the interview for this book. He didn't just pick some of his stories. He filtered those more relevant in this context. Besides stating the facts, he also extracted the *gems* (his learning) from each of those stories.

✓ Introverts are good at writing

While verbal communication might not suit introverts very

well, writing does. Before you discard writing—if you don't believe that's your strength—keep in mind that there are several writing styles.

It seems that formal and business writing styles suit Alex well, taken into consideration the written communication he had to produce during his first job. But he might be good at other writing styles as well.

√ Introverts are strategic; they think about consequences

Alex's perspective on leadership: *you need to be aware of the social and economic issues related to the project.* Charisma is not enough.

He's always well prepared, which requires strategic thinking, research, and thinking about the consequences. Which feeds back into the research that helps him to prepare better. Not to mention his strategic way of using his strengths to move his career forward.

√ Introverts are big thinkers

They are motivated by causes that have a bigger, more positive impact in the world.

Alex's passion for making a positive impact on people on a larger scale shows up in his thinking and the examples he chose to share with us.

List of Introverts' Strengths covered in this book:
gabrielacasineanu.com/list-introverts-strengths

Chapter Three

MIHAELA

If you think that you know what you want to do, you'll shape yourself to be the person that you think you want to be. But if you just keep yourself open, you'll shape yourself to be who you are—not who you think you want to be.

— MIHAELA STAMATE

I've been using social media—the introvert's way—since 2006 (when I started my coaching business). My following has grown to a point where I haven't had the chance to meet all of my Facebook friends yet. So imagine my pleasant surprise when Mihaela said that she came from 100 km away at my first "Meet the Author" event for the book *Introverts: Leverage Your Strengths for an Effective Job Search*. So we finally met in person!

That's what one of the things I love about that book: it helps introverts step out and connect! We're not shy all the time as we're often portrayed! Many times when I have a booth with that book I get introverts coming to me, and we have great conversations!

Like other introverts I've interviewed for this book, Mihaela agreed to share something about herself just because I asked and it might help other introverts! We love to help others if you didn't notice this yet! :-)

At one point, Mihaela wanted to back off because she thought that she didn't provide enough value. I'll let you figure out if she did, I personally like what she shared with us!

Gabriela: Mihaela, tell us about one of your biggest life challenges and what helped you to overcome it.

Mihaela: One of the challenges I have is expressing in words what I think. Being an introvert, I spend a lot of time by myself and I don't think in words. I think in sensations and images, anything but words! It's a really big challenge for me to express something in a coherent manner. Because of this, I tend to avoid conversations with all my strength. But I've also noticed that if I am in a limited situation, I can just go and I have to come up with something! I try to put myself into situations like these, jumping head first.

For example, I started volunteering and I had to meet people. But I was doing that knowing that I'm helping others. This made it easier for me to connect with people and made it meaningful to talk to them...[she got emotional at this point.]

Gabriela: It's okay. I like that emotions are bubbling up. If you want to weave them into the story it's even better. That's how people connect: it's something deeper than just words.

Mihaela: It's something that I really struggled with, and I still struggle. And in order to fix it or solve it, I have to push myself outside my comfort zone, and it's always scary.

When I started volunteering, I had to meet people, talk to them, and explain what I'm doing and why. That's what helped me not to be afraid of people anymore.

Another challenge was starting my own business as a massage therapist. Before that, I worked in the corporate world for about 13 years. I always had problems during meetings, like I couldn't talk! Or when I would talk, my voice was strangled, and I just couldn't say what I was thinking. Everything would go blank, like I would see black in front of my eyes and I wouldn't remember what I said, although I had a plan beforehand of what I wanted to say.

When I started my own business, and I had to talk to the clients, it was hard at the beginning because I didn't know how to do it. On the other hand, it was also somehow easier because I was in a position of helping them, and it was a one-on-one connection. It wasn't me against a bunch of other people to which I couldn't connect at the same time. When I need to talk to a small group or with one person, that's the best! And again, I forced myself to do it. I think this is something that happens over and over again: I have to force myself to do something that is outside my comfort zone. First, I try to become aware of what my problem is, and then I push through it.

Gabriela: Did you notice any progress in time?

Mihaela: Yes, right now I'm a lot better with my clients. I'm not afraid anymore. I'm still a bit nervous when I have a first-time client, but not too much, and definitely not with my existing clients! It's very funny: one of my clients came last week, and at the end of the session she said: "That was an amazing session! I liked both the treatment and the conversation."

You know, talking seemed to be my weakness. But at the same time, when it's something meaningful, I can talk! So, I think that's the difference.

Gabriela: That's really good! You gave us two examples, and I love that one is in the corporate world. The other, in your own business, when you take the time to talk with people about something meaningful. You already covered some of the introvert characteristics.

Mihaela: I guess…

Gabriela: First of all, we're not good at talking to many people, especially when you find yourself in a formal situation where you're in the spotlight. But we're good at talking one-on-one, which happens in your business.

We're also good at finding the strength to get out of our comfort zone when it's something meaningful to us. That's what you're doing in your business! You did the same thing with volunteering and found your own reasons to push yourself.

Introverts find motivation from inside when they have a meaningful objective or need to talk about a meaningful topic. While volunteering, you found a meaningful objective and you were able to overcome all the other communication challenges of being a volunteer. So, you use your strengths very well!

Mihaela: Thank you!

Gabriela: I asked if there is any progress because I want the readers to know that you don't just push, push, push...

Mihaela: No, it becomes easier. It's true. I don't know if it's because I believe more in myself now or if it's just like everything else in the world: you need practice. I believe that if you practice enough times it can become more like a second nature.

Gabriela: You expand your comfort zone.

Mihaela: Exactly.

Gabriela: And the more you do it, the more you get used to it. Like you're saying, it becomes like second nature; a new habit.

Mihaela: What helped me also was having a best friend. I discovered her late in my life, and we became really close. I think we were in our early forties, and we started talking almost every day. She's an extrovert, but also intuitive and feeling (NF). That's what connects us very well. She has the same challenge as me: she cannot always put in words what she thinks. But because we had to talk to each other, and we had to express what we were feeling, we were able to create that habit of transforming thoughts into words. We also knew that we are understood and accepted unconditionally. I think this really helps me: to have someone who understands me and accepts me.

Gabriela: What you are saying: it feels good to be in a nurturing environment. It allows you to open up.

Mihaela: Exactly! Supportive and nurturing. A nurturing environment can mean different things. But that specific way of nurturing, where you talk to somebody, gives you a chance to express what you're feeling, and you feel understood unconditionally. That's what helped me overcome that specific problem: not being able to put into words what I'm thinking.

Gabriela: That's great! May I ask what was your experience before you switched to your business? You said you worked in the corporate world.

Mihaela: When I was working in the corporate world, I was really afraid of everything. For example, when I was crossing the plant, I was hoping that nobody would see me. I was trying my best just to be invisible! And whenever somebody would come and talk to me, I would feel almost like under attack because I was not comfortable being seen at all.

What was the intent of your question?

Gabriela: It was about something different, but I like what you're saying. I'm ok with whatever comes up from this discussion, and you brought up something very interesting: introverts often feel that they just want to be in their own world, not seen by others, or be in the spotlight.

My question came from curiosity: I was wondering in what profession you were in before starting your business.

Mihaela: I'm a textile engineer, but in Romania, I couldn't find a job as a textile engineer. So what I did, and it was a very uncharacteristic approach for me, I went and talked to a manager in the steel factory because my diploma project was about protective clothing. I asked him if he can give me an idea of how much he pays for the protective clothing he's using over a year, and I'll try to come up with a plan to show him how he can save money. Because that was part of what we did in school: we learned to make patterns, but also to design a production line from scratch. So, I did my part and showed him that if he would invest a specific amount of money, within two or three years, he will make everything back, and from then he'll be making a profit! He was very interested in the idea, and he approved the project. Unfortunately, the company started having major financial problems soon after. Everything went downhill, and the project was canceled, but they kept me in the marketing department. From there I had the chance to be offered training in quality assurance. I did this training, and then I became an internal quality auditor. Then the department I worked with was dissolved, and I was offered a position with the archives.

In the meantime, I found a textile company who needed somebody with quality assurance training to build their quality assurance program, which I did.

At the same time, while looking for alternative employment options, I applied to immigrate to Canada, and a year after, my immigration application was approved. I moved to Canada, and I was hired as a quality technician. One of the interviewers was curious about why I applied for that position because I was overqualified. I told him that my plan is to start from the bottom and understand things from the bottom up, hoping that I'll be able to grow within the company. I was hired to do mechanical and electrical sample evaluations. At one point the company slowly started moving their production to China. Unfortunately, the recession came, and there were major layoffs at the company I was working for. I was one of the many people who lost their jobs.

Gabriela: Now I'm curious. When you look back at your life, with all the professional experiences you've been through in different industries, how has it helped you to become the person who you are right now?

Mihaela: Well, I think that working in various fields helped me become a better professional. Right now, I'm a massage therapist. I think that studying to be an engineer made my brain more organized and that really helped me. I needed that type of structure, and I carried it with me in a direction that is more people-oriented.

Gabriela: And it's helping?

Mihaela: It is! I believe that my ability to synthesize things comes from there. Working in quality assurance also helped me to be okay with mistakes, by understanding that only when you identify one you can change it! There are things that you can do to improve when you find an error, so discovering it is not a bad thing.

When I was working in quality control, and I was finding mistakes in what others were doing, I would try to put them in a way that they wouldn't feel guilty. Because as I said before, in order to change something, you first have to identify and admit it. If you are hiding it, it will never change. I think that's what helped me, although I still struggle to accept my own mistakes. I find it easier to accept other people's mistakes, I don't know why. I have to keep reminding myself that it's okay to make mistakes.

Gabriela: Great! I have a similar background to you: going through different professions, including quality assurance. That's why I asked the question about how it shaped the person you are right now. And I also want introverts to understand that I didn't need to know my life's purpose from the beginning; there wasn't a straight line toward it.

You can go left, then right...and take it from there if you want.

Mihaela: That's exactly what I was talking about yesterday to my daughter, who is in grade nine. She feels the pressure of finding what she wants in life because she has a few friends and at least two of them apparently know exactly what they want to do. I told her: "If you think that you know at this age what you want to do, you'll shape yourself to be the person that you think you want to be. But if you just keep yourself open, you'll shape yourself to be who you are, not who you think you want to be."

Gabriela: Oh, I love that!

Mihaela: I believe that it's important for her not to feel the pressure of becoming something, but to see what she is to become!

Gabriela: Well said! I love everything you've said so far. You started with your challenge about transforming thoughts into words, and how volunteering and having a best friend helped you. Then you talked about the different professional directions you've been through. Thank you so much!

Mihaela: You're welcome!

Gabriela: I'm curious now: what did you get out of this discussion so far?

Mihaela: Well, I think it's again challenging my fear of being noticed. I pushed myself to do this interview because I was afraid of doing it. And what I learned is that I'm not by myself in this struggle. I belong to a group. There are other people who experience the same challenges...and it's okay!

Gabriela: And there are many of us. In Susan Cain's book

Quiet, she mentions that 40 percent of the US population are introverts. Forty percent!!! So, it's not just a small group. What we call *struggles* comes from comparing ourselves—like you're saying—with the *standard* of being extroverted. But actually, I see extroverts and introverts like Yin and Yang.

Mihaela: Exactly!

Gabriela: So it's not that we're better or worse than them (the extroverts). We're good as we are, we just have to understand how to overcome our own challenges by using our strengths.

Introverts are smart, they are strategic thinkers, they can see the big picture. And if we understand ourselves better and start using these strengths more often, we can help society more. But if we're comparing ourselves with extroverts, it's like: "Oh, I'm less than them...so I better stay in my own bubble!"

Mihaela: It's a shame that I felt like that a lot, at least in the company I worked in. The majority of the people who were in executive positions were extroverts. And for them, it's hard to see how an introvert thinks, feels, and functions. I wish that people accepted each other more than they do. Because as you said, there are strengths in the extroverts and there are strengths in the introverts too. Everybody can bring something different, and that makes a whole. Not just a half, you know?

Gabriela: I agree. In another interview I did recently, someone came up with the same idea: that maybe I should go out and raise more people's awareness. I guess my first step is to help introverts understand themselves better, what their strengths are, and how to use them more efficiently.

Probably the next step will be to go to groups and companies to talk about both, like you're saying, so extroverts better understand the introverts, and each of us (introverts) better understands the extroverts. Because we can't say we understand the extroverts well either. We understand they're not like us, but we don't know more.

Mihaela: That's a great idea. I feel like the earlier it starts, the better the outcome would be. If you teach kids and teenagers about that, you'll change the world faster than teaching adults, who are already set in their ways. It's harder to change adults than it is to change kids. Kids can be inspired by things like these much easier.

Gabriela: It's funny you're saying that. The other interviewee came up with the same idea, and it's not the first time I heard that I should go toward kids and teenagers with what I'm doing.

Mihaela: Absolutely. I think it's a great idea! You told me the other day that you were able to catch a teenage guy's interest for two hours with your workshop. I'm pretty sure that you inspired him! Although you said that he was not participating *per se*, his brain and his heart were participating in it, I'm sure. Sometimes, especially introverts, they just remember one thing, one word or one idea...and then they go home and they keep thinking about it. And that reminds me of another thing that helped me: music. Listening to music, actually the combination of lyrics and music, helped me associate words to some of my feelings. And then starting from there, I was able to build, to come up with something more coherent. I had a base to build on: starting with a phrase from a song, I would think of my own experience around that problem. And that helped me. Sometimes, because I don't think in words, it's such a big mess in my head that it's hard to find the starting point. And that gave me a starting point.

Gabriela: That's very interesting. Thank you so much!

Some of the introvert strengths I've noticed in Mihaela's interview without repeating too much of what was said in the previous chapters:

√ Introverts express themselves in various ways

Mihaela thinks in images, sensations, movements…anything but words! When she learned to put her thoughts into words, she improved her verbal communication. Music helped her too, to make connections and build the bridge to verbal communication.

Her way of thinking is different but not less than others'. By having access to those non-verbal ways of thinking, her ability to see the world may enrich the perspective of other people who are not able to think in the same way.

√ For a meaningful cause, introverts are willing to learn how to be better communicators

To feel her need to connect with others and help (them and herself), Mihaela joined forces with her great friend to help each other learn how to express themselves and communicate better.

√ Introverts find creative ways to overcome challenges

Mihaela threw herself into volunteering to force herself to

improve her verbal communication, and in the process, she learned to *swim* (she found ways to do it). Then she started applying the learning in other challenging situations as well.

✓ Introverts are assertive when they believe in their ideas

Although it was not natural to her, Mihaela found the courage to approach and present to a manager her innovative idea, after well preparing her argument, and won him over.

It was assertiveness at work since introverts don't feel comfortable in front of people they consider an authority (a manager, for example).

✓ Introverts are willing to plan ahead to minimize risks

Mihaela took the time to prepare for the meetings she had to attend because she knew that verbal communication wasn't her strength, so she couldn't rely on finding the right message on the spot.

✓ Introverts are (very) sensitive

In some situations, this might be perceived as a weakness, like Mihaela's reaction when she tried to speak in that meeting.

But being sensitive can also be a strength: that's where the empathy and compassion come from! Mihaela redirected her professional path toward a field where this characteristic is highly valued: becoming a massage therapist.

✓ Introverts can distance themselves from a situation and design a generic problem-solving process

Mihaela realized that she first needs to become aware of

what her problem is > Then what she needs to focus on > Find the courage to push through (focusing on a meaningful reason) > Learns from that experience > Applies the process whenever and how often it's needed > It gets better in time > Becomes a second nature!

In other words: applying this process to herself > makes *being out of the comfort zone* a prerequisite for an *expanded comfort zone* > which becomes the *new comfort zone.*

√ Introverts are stimulated by a supportive and nurturing environment

Having a best friend helped Mihaela to open up more, learn, and improve. Also, it made her feel understood and accepted, which is often difficult for introverts.

On the contrary, the technical field environment she worked in previously, where she was surrounded by many extroverts, was making her uncomfortable, afraid, feeling under attack, and she had a tendency to hide (instead of opening up). So choosing the right environment is very important for the well-being of an introvert.

√ Introverts feel the need to belong

Although they often withdraw or isolate themselves, which helps them recharge and reflect, they also feel the need to be part of something; a community of like-minded people, who understand them.

Learning that there are other people who share the same traits—other introverts—made Mihaela feel good that she's not alone anymore.

√ Introverts are resilient and adaptable

Life pushed Mihaela to change career directions several times (textile engineering, marketing specialist, internal quality auditor). She did well since the first company she worked for moved her to the Marketing department when they started to have financial problems, then again—instead of laying her off—they trained her in quality assurance and become an internal auditor.

Yet, she found herself more peaceful only when she chose a direction that better suited her personality and style (massage therapist). She was also able to transfer some skills developed in the previous professions (being structured, organized) to help her with the new direction (her massage therapist business).

A word of caution: just because introverts can adapt to any position—and make an effort to perform well—it doesn't mean that it won't take a toll on them if they stay too long in inappropriate role.

✓ Introverts put themselves in the others' *shoes*

Mihaela thought about the employer's perspective before the job interview—his concerns about her being overqualified, for example—which helped her come up with answers that addressed those concerns and landed her the job.

✓ Introverts are caring and willing to support others

While working in quality assurance, Mihaela was careful about how she spoke with people. She made them understand their mistakes and how to correct them, instead of making them feel guilty.

Yet, introverts are sometimes too harsh with themselves (perfectionists?) or struggle to accept their own errors. But they learn and get better at it because they strive to perform well.

✓ Introverts are deep thinkers *and love to share their insights*

They're interested in things beyond the material world and are tapping into their inner wisdom to get answers—see Mihaela's wise advice for her daughter about her life purpose.

Yet they prefer to speak only with those with whom they have a good connection or are willing to listen.

✓ Introverts are capable of seeing beyond the fear and push through it

Mihaela's ability to find something meaningful and push through came up several times in her stories. For example: while volunteering and in communication with her first clients.

This ability is enhanced when you reframe or re-label the situation and look for the meaningful purpose—beyond the fear—which gives introverts the courage and energy for the breakthrough. The fear is often a reflection of the skills that needs to be learned or improved.

List of Introverts' Strengths
covered in this book
gabrielacasineanu.com/list-introverts-strengths

Chapter Four

GERARD

One of the things that kept me going was my continuous learning. Like being out and active...meeting people and making connections to learn or see. That's how I digested what networking really is and how I could do it strategically to my benefit.

— GERARD KELEDJIAN

As you'll notice, Gerard also found a *trick* that helps him get out of his comfort zone for a meaningful cause, which—in his case—impacts more people!

I met Gerard a few years ago, but we didn't stay in touch. We happened to meet again at a job fair when our booths faced each other. I was showcasing my first book, and he was representing the Canada-wide TV show, New Canadians TV, that he's been producing for over three years to help new immigrants and wannabe Canadians succeed faster.

"I'm an introvert too," said Gerard approaching my booth, curious to find out more about my book. He ended up interviewing me for New Canadians TV, and we've collaborated a few times since.

I found it really interesting how he was able to turn his struggling immigrant story into a successful TV and web show watched all over Canada and abroad...especially knowing that he's an introvert! He's also an immigrant entrepreneurship booster, but that's another story. :-)

So I didn't miss the chance to *force* this Armenian-Canadian to share his challenges with us, even if that meant asking questions that *pulled* the stories out of a...still shy introvert!

Gabriela: Gerard, you mentioned earlier that you changed since you came to Canada. What was the change about? And why did you feel the need to change?

Gerard: Canada is a different country from where I came from, and obviously, a different environment requires something different. Some of the changes happened naturally, without me realizing that I'd changed. For others, I realized that I needed to change because I had to adapt to the new environment to become effective.

For example, one change that happened was networking. Networking for me was already a new concept by itself. Now that I know how to network, if I look back, to Lebanon or Dubai, where I worked for a while before moving to Canada, I never strategically networked. I just built my network over time through my classmates, colleagues, friends, and relatives. So here I needed to build that network. One way to do that was to approach people just to meet for coffee—what you call an informational interview. One of the people I met this way was the publisher of the Toronto Star after someone suggested that I email him to meet. Back home or in Dubai, I would have never thought of doing something similar because the editor of the leading national newspaper there would not even read your email. Or if they read, they're like: "Who's this idiot who dares to ask me for a meeting? Do I have time for him?"

But here I met. Just the fact of meeting him and others, such as the news directors of CBC News and 680 News, was a new concept for me. I even became creative in meeting people. Someone told me that I need to meet the news director of City News, but he didn't give me the email address. And I was shy to ask him for her email address. I knew that City News was part of the Rogers media group, and I also knew that they have one format for email addresses. Since I had the email address of another person working at Rogers, I guessed the email address of City News' news director and sent her a message. She replied, and we met.

This concept of approaching people just to meet was new to me, but I had to do it in Canada because I was trying to achieve a breakthrough. Having a media background, I was aiming to connect to the local media industry, though eventually, I went more towards the immigration sector.

Another thing about networking: in all my life I had never been to an event where I didn't know at least one person. Even if I knew someone at an event, I never went alone; there always had to be at least someone, always going together. In Canada, I even traveled to an event alone. About six months after being in Canada, I learned that one of the main media organizations was having their annual conference in Halifax, Nova Scotia. I booked a ticket and flew to that three-day conference without knowing anyone there. Theoretically, it was challenging for me. I didn't know what to expect, but I said to myself: "I'm going!" Worst-case scenario, I was going to pay for the conference and get nothing out of it; just going and attending the conference and coming back. Or I could see parts of Halifax. However, what helped me was the fact that the conference was in a hotel, and somehow you're *stuck* there. So during the coffee breaks, and before or after the conference sessions, you had to be with people. So I met and talked; it was a learning experience.

Gabriela: How did you approach people at the conference to talk to them?

Gerard: During the panel discussions or the breakout sessions, the panelists introduced themselves. So if someone was of interest to me, I approached that person after the session. I looked for at least one person on each panel discussion to approach. I approached the panelist I could relate to the most or maybe they said something that I could use: "Hey, you spoke about...and this is something I want to know more about."

Or if they were talking about news, I said: "I'm new to Canada and I've worked in the news environment..." So without someone teaching me, I tried to find something in common when approaching people.

Gabriela: That is natural to introverts. When they have something meaningful in mind, they find the motivation to go for it.

Gerard: At that point I was already doing those coffee

meetings or just sending emails to people to explain that I'm new to the country, saying: "I'm a media professional, can we meet? Or just talk about the industry?"

I never asked for jobs, however, I was putting pressure on myself to come out of the meeting with "something" and usually it doesn't happen like that. Just the fact that the meeting happened was something to celebrate. But if nothing came out of the meeting, that brought me down. For example, when I met the publisher of the Toronto Star... how do I take that forward?

Sometimes I showed them my resume (at the conference, for example) and asked: "Is there anything that I need to change?"

"Your resume is good," they replied, but then I was thinking in the back of my mind: "Okay, then why is it not working?"

Gabriela: What stopped you from asking that question?

Gerard: Maybe the fact that I'm shy as a person. I was able to overcome the shyness to approach a person, but then I didn't take a step forward to ask why I'm not getting interviews?

Gabriela: Where are you now regarding networking?

Gerard: Now I'm a very good networker, and I even have a nickname for that: Connector. People see me as a connector, as I'm very good at connecting people, whether in-person or virtually. When I see there might be a common interest with someone, even if I haven't spoken to you, I make the connection. Many times, something fruitful has come out of the connections I've made. Funny that sometimes people forget that I connected them, so they don't say "Thank you." Once

I connected two people at an event I organized, and after a year, one of them was showing off: "Hey, we're working together." I didn't tell him that I connected them. I don't know, sometimes I want to say something, but I don't know the best or nicest way to say it. Maybe I could say: "I'm glad you met at the event I organized," maybe they'll remember that I played a role initiating their connection.

Today, I go to events where I don't know anyone—it's not a challenge for me anymore. I don't have a challenge approaching people unless the setting of the event is very restrictive. Like one of the events I went to recently, they had these round tables and it was packed. The tables were too close to each other, and you couldn't move around. The two people that ended up sitting next to me were very irrelevant. There was nothing in common between us, they couldn't get anything from me and I didn't see anything that I could get from them. You can (and should) still network in such situations, but professionally you don't take anything from there. In a couple of minutes, you would know if they might be irrelevant or they might have someone or something to share. In the example I told you, since it was very difficult to move around, I ended up being "stuck" with the two people around me, and I just talked for the sake of talking. In similar events, or in events held in pubs or meetings around a long table where it's not easy to see or talk with everyone, you can only talk with the two or three people around you. But in conferences and events with open spaces, I'm good at approaching people. I'm not shy now; if there's someone I want to meet, I go and talk to them directly. One example is when I approached the first sponsor of New Canadians TV. I was trying hard to get seed funding to launch the TV show. And I had approached a bank and others, but I couldn't get any sponsorship funding. Then one day I was at a diversity-related event, and one of the panelists was the Dean of The Chang School at Ryerson University. I thought that The Chang School is a good candidate to approach, so I approached her. She mentioned that she was a former Minister of Citizenship and Immigration, so immediately she realized the value of New Canadians TV. At that time, she was still interim dean and she said: "If I get confirmed, I'd like to meet again and take this further." So, I started following The Chang School's news to see if/when the dean was going to be confirmed. In about a month she was confirmed. I waited a week, then emailed her and we met.

Now I'm not afraid to meet or approach by email people that I haven't met if I can get their email address or contact info —even from articles sometimes. Yesterday I was reading an article about one of the regions in Ontario that is looking to increase their visibility with new immigrants. The person's email was below the article, so I put it on my list to email her this week. I don't know what comes out of it, but I'll approach her. Worst case, they will know about New Canadians TV if they don't know it yet. Twitter helps me a lot in connecting to people now.

Gabriela: In what way? How are you using Twitter to connect with people?

Gerard: Now LinkedIn as well, but initially Twitter. You can use Twitter in different ways; I started with following people, and some of them followed back. Sometimes I used to comment, not too much. I could have done much more. One person, for example, she was an instructor at Durham College, and we connected on Twitter. I don't remember how, but for about a year we followed each other. I think I had replied to something she had posted. After a year I invited her to be a guest speaker at an event I organized for internationally-educated media professionals. We met, and there was no need to break the ice because we even forgot that it was the first time we'd met in person because we'd had one year of interaction. Now I'm also very active on LinkedIn—more than Twitter I would say. Many people know me or know about me, but we don't have a direct connection. So, when it comes to connecting, it's easier to approach them, pitch them something, or just meet. Because they already know about you, you don't need to build that trust because they've seen you for a while, they've followed your activities. Being active on social media helps me in my work and to make connections.

Gabriela: I think that's enough from the networking part. Let's talk about something else. You got the idea of New Canadians TV at one point. How did you go from the idea to start taking baby steps…getting to where it is right now— three years after—a TV show broadcast all over Canada and a web show with many visitors from abroad?

Gerard: The initial idea for New Canadians TV (it was a different name) came when I realized that I need to get my local media experience in Canada. I had years of media experience from overseas, but I realized that I needed to do something in Canada that people could probably relate to more or they could check back if they needed to. That rein- forced the idea that I need to do something. I started looking for volunteer opportunities, which landed me at Rogers TV, the community channel at Rogers Media. The volunteer opportunities there were very basic, and you couldn't progress, so they didn't lead me to where I wanted to be. Then, by chance, I realized that I could pitch my own show to the community channel and produce it. When I realized that's an opportunity for me, I pitched. Because it was a volunteer position and I was not going to get paid, I decided that it had to be something I am passionate about. By that time, four or five months had already passed of me being in Canada, and I had made some mistakes, with one of them particularly being very big. It made me lose confidence in myself and doubt my judgment for over a year.

Gabriela: That's an interesting point, what helped you bounce back?

Gerard: I realized that I could use my storytelling and media skills. There was a gap in TV programming in regard to newcomers. So I realized that I could use my skills to help myself build my Canadian media experience, while at the same time help other new immigrants get introduced to the resources that I didn't know earlier: networking, mentoring, and all the services offered by the immigrant associations and employment service providers that I was learning about.

This was the initial goal. Initially, I didn't think of it as a long-term program because the community channel where I was volunteering used to give only short-term production opportunities. They offered to help me produce six episodes, so that was the original plan.

Because they started seeing me as the person who combines media skills and immigration knowledge; and has a big network of contacts in the immigration sector, that volunteering experience landed me a job with an immigrant-related website.

In the meantime, the community channel offered me continued airtime, but they wanted me to produce it myself, as they needed to dedicate their own resources to new members of the community. I too had the desire to continue producing the TV show for newcomers because of how well it was received and was impactful, but I had to figure out how.

I started working for that immigrant-related website, thinking that somehow, I might be able to produce my show. I worked there for about three years, but I realized that I was not able to use all my skills. Actually, it was making me feel *depressed* or down for different reasons. There were moments when I felt reborn as soon as I stepped out of the office; I felt I was a different person. In the office, I was very sad—somehow *depressed*—not because I was working for someone else but because I felt they were not really helping immigrants! They were very money-focused and liked to do only things that will generate money, while I thought that there were other things that newcomers needed, that we could do, and which won't cost us any extra money, while at the same time helping us make money in the long-term.

That's why I kept that dream alive: to produce my TV show for newcomers! After finally deciding that I wanted to produce it, I started to actively seek money to fund the production. When I finally got the funding I needed, I relaunched the TV show, giving it a new name to reflect the new nature of the program: national, across Canada…and of course, I left my job with the immigrant-related website!

I always believed in balancing the business and the social aspects of my work. Now, I could still make money but also genuinely help people.

Gabriela: Great! Now back to my previous question. What

helped you to bounce back when you were down, before producing the first series and finding that job?

Gerard: It's a complicated picture, I would say. Even myself, I don't understand it sometimes. As if I was two different people at the same time: from the inside I was very down, while from the outside I kept an image of a very strong person.

For one year I was freelancing for an industry magazine. They used to pay me $300 for one article a month but obviously that didn't pay my bills, was not enough to survive. But I wasn't under an immediate pressure of generating money, so I always said I'm working and showed that I'm working. It didn't matter that I was writing just one article a month. Whenever I was with people, I was saying that I'm writing for this industry magazine. But from the inside, I was not confident because the more time was passing, the more I was seeing that there's no light at the end of the tunnel and that the tunnel was getting longer! At some point, I even didn't know what I could do to come out of it.

One of the things that kept me going was my continuous learning. Like being out and active, going to events, going to meetups...meeting people and making connections to learn or see, and that's how I digested what networking really is and how I could do it strategically to my benefit.

One more thing about networking: it's not just exchanging business cards, you have to know how to network authentically so that you can benefit out of it.

Gabriela: Did it happen gradually?

Gerard: I think it happened gradually. One thing that helped, as I said earlier, was my continuous learning.

Another thing that helped: when the initial TV show I produced as a volunteer was aired, people started to see me as a success story. That gave me a nice feeling, although from the inside I wasn't believing in my success. I didn't see myself being successful because I wasn't making money. It was good to produce the TV show, similar to writing a book, but you're distributing it for free. People are congratulating you, but no single dollar is entering your pocket. At the end of the day, I needed to pay three dollars for the TTC ticket to take the subway and go back home. People were seeing me as successful, but I wasn't seeing myself that way or I wasn't believing that it was a solid success. It was a nice success, but a "fragile" one.

Another thing is that I planted good seeds in good soil, and eventually I got a good harvest; I made good connections. Maybe I was lucky, but I found myself at events or places where I was able to make good connections and eventually those connections helped me establish myself and move forward in Canada.

Gabriela: Do you trust your intuition?

Gerard: Yes, I do. If I believe in something or like it, even if I don't see a direct or immediate benefit, I go for it. If I feel something is good, I need to go for it.

Initially, I was at a point when I had lots of time, so I didn't worry about selecting or choosing. Obviously, now I don't have as much free time, so I have to choose. Let's say, today I chose not to go to a certain event because I didn't want to *waste* half a day on just one event. I wanted to meet you for an hour or an hour and a half, then do some work at home. Earlier if I were free, I would have gone to the event, maybe rescheduling your meeting to earlier or later, if needed.

Gabriela: Would you say that right now you're more selective?

Gerard: Yes, most likely for one reason: I have less free time now. So I have to select. Second, being out there all the time leaves you with no time to work on anything, even to follow up with the business cards you collected. You need time to write emails, right? Like yesterday: I had registered for an event, but I decided to cancel because I realized that the day before I was out at a meeting, today I'm meeting you...and the week is over, I haven't done anything! Yesterday's event was not directly related to me so I could afford to skip it because I needed time for myself.

Gabriela: How often do you go to events?

Gerard: Before I used to go to three, four events a week. Now I'm having more business meetings, so when it comes to events, I'm more selective: I focus on immigration-related events, so I filter out other events. There are events that I'll probably benefit from personally, but professionally if I don't see a connection, I filter them out. Plus, location counts as well—like yesterday's event, another reason why I didn't go. Initially, I was thinking that I will have the day free, then I got stuck with a project and ended up working full-day. Waiting for three hours after the project work was done, then attending the event, then going home to Pickering would be too much. I know the person may be upset that I didn't go, but what can I do? Myself, I'm important as well.

Gabriela: Did you send a message to the person that something came up?

Gerard: Yesterday I didn't send. I know I should've done so, but I didn't.

Gabriela: You've said many interesting things so far.

Gerard: One other thing I'd like to point out, a *trick* that I do. I'm not outgoing, and I don't like to speak at events or sit on panels. But because I know in Canada this is a must—you have to be seen as an expert, you have to be out there to build trust in yourself—whenever there's a speaking opportunity, immediately I say *"Yes"* if it's relevant! Then I regret, but by the time I regret it's already too late, so I force myself to be in front of people.

Gabriela: Did you noticed that gradually it becomes easier?

Gerard: Speaking got easier. I know the first time I spoke publicly in Canada, my mouth got so dry, and I was too shy to ask for water. There was water on the table, but I was the last panelist from the podium and the jar was far from where I was. I didn't think that I would need water. And I couldn't say in the middle of my talk "Hey just a minute, let me fill my glass." Now when I speak, I don't have that issue anymore: either I have water nearby, or I don't have the dryness because I'm less stressed. I will still have that anxiety before I'm called to the podium, but the moment I'm out and I know that I can't backtrack, I'm okay.

Gabriela: Did you do anything to get rid of that anxiety?

Gerard: No, I don't think I can get rid of it. I mean it's natural; even when people go live on radio interviews, there is some anxiety. It will decrease with practice, or maybe you'll be better at managing that anxiety, but there will still be some. So far I'm fine. It's not that my turn to speak has come and I can't get words out of my mouth. No, I'm fine. So, my *trick* is putting myself in the situation, and then worry about it!

Gabriela: Did it happen to you, with the public speaking, to see someone else speaking and think: *Oh, I could do a better speech on the same topic?*

Gerard: Yes, because it's always easier to be on the other side. Like playing a soccer game: it's easier to criticize the player, but when you're the player the situation is different.

Gabriela: I'm coming from another perspective. Because I see that introverts have a lot of good ideas, and they hold them for themselves.

Gerard: Not with public speaking. I have that problem with questions during meetings or in the Q&A sessions (when people ask questions). I always think about my question so much that either this opportunity closes (no more questions allowed) or someone else asks the same question that I had. Sometimes I overthink, like how to ask the question. Other times I think: that's not a good question to ask. But then someone asks it, and they like the question, and I feel bad that I had that same question...why didn't I ask it? So, it's a good question, why I thought that it's not a good question?

Gabriela: I like everything you said, thank you!

Gerard: Pleasure!

Gabriela: See, I made you talk! :-)

By now, you've probably started noticing more easily how the introvert strengths show up in these stories.

Let me list some of those that I noticed in Gerard's interview:

✓ Introverts can see and connect unnoticed *dots* to create a new project

Reflecting on his own experience—struggling to find work experience in his field as a new immigrant—Gerard was able to identify a gap: *there are useful services and programs for newcomers and many stories of successful immigrants, but newcomers are not aware of them.*

Then he realized how his *skills and experience* in media and journalism could *bridge that gap* to make that information available to newcomers so that they can succeed faster.

✓ Introverts are visionary

What started as a small project based on a need and Gerard's passion—to help new immigrants get introduced to the resources he didn't know about earlier—became a dream that is still unfolding; creating a bigger impact with every year passing by.

✓ Introverts are assertive

Knowing what his objective as a newcomer was (to gain Canadian experience in his field), Gerard assertively looked for helpful information and opportunities. That's how he learned what works in the new professional environment: networking, mentoring, gaining work experience through volunteering, etc. He applied these strategies to create and continually expand his network, and find relevant volunteering opportunities for him.

Another example of assertiveness: after meeting a potential sponsor for New Canadians TV, he patiently waited for her to be confirmed in the new position, then he reached out to her again (being able to secure the first funding for his program).

✓ Introverts are creative

Besides using his creativity in media and journalism, Gerard also became creative in finding what he wanted. For example, guessing an email address based on the company's email format led him to the person he was looking for. The project idea pitched to the community TV channel also reflects his creativity.

✓ With a clear objective in mind, introverts can get over the inner barriers

Despite being a shy introvert who never went to events by himself before, Gerard started to go to conferences in his field because he really wanted to connect with people in his industry! Then, after he started to produce New Canadians TV, he continued to *network strategically* to help the program grow and become more impactful.

Noticing the positive effect of networking on his business, he made it a self-imposed *have to*. And in the process, he discovered which approach worked for him: select relevant conferences, connect with panelists he resonates with, and attend events with enough space to move around (to increase the chance of connecting with people who could help him advance on his path). Gerard perfected his networking style so much that someone said recently: "I would never have guessed that Gerard is an introvert!"

✓ Introverts are open and flexible

Initially, Gerard thought that getting back to his field (media and journalism) was what he needed, but he openly embraced the new direction—applying his skills in the immigration sector—and surrendered to his powerful dream. He realized that media and journalism could actually become tools to create a bigger, more meaningful impact.

✓ Introverts are gentle people

While meeting people over a coffee, Gerard didn't pressure his contacts to help him (even if he wanted to get back in his field). He used the same approach with people he met through social media (Twitter and LinkedIn) or when sending an email to someone listed in a published article.

✓ Introverts are genuine in building relationships

Following up on his gentle approach when meeting someone for the first time, Gerard genuinely built those relationships in time. Noticing that his approach was working, he continued to use it up to the point that his shyness was no longer showing up while he strategically connected and built professional relationships.

✓ Introverts like a long-term approach

Instead of *hit-and-run*, Gerard's long-term approach when it comes to building relationships helps New Canadians TV and his business overall. Remember the Durham College instructor he connected with on Twitter? Later, he was able to bring her as a guest speaker to an event.

A focus on continuously expanding your network and genuinely building relationships is an approach that works well for introverts. The very nature of social media makes it a great tool to use for this purpose.

✓ Introverts understand the power of the *win-win* approach

Introverts love collaboration. And their respect for others leads to building relationships for mutual benefit (win-win).

Gerard's nickname "Connector" shows his ability to identify mutual interest and his willingness to help others—qualities embedded in the win-win approach, which has a boomerang effect (it helps him as well).

✓ Introverts' self-talk is a strength

While it could also be a weakness (if you focus on the negative self-talk), Gerard was able to use it in a positive way. He thinks of a positive *worst-case scenario* to push himself out of his comfort zone—like when he wanted to go by himself to a conference (*he could see parts of Halifax*). Or when he sent an email for a potential collaboration to someone who didn't know him (*at least he'll know about New Canadians TV*).

Actually, the science shows that positive self-talk can decrease stress and is effective even for people dealing with anxiety.

✓ Magic happens when introverts trust their intuition

By trusting his intuition—whether choosing what events to attend or to follow his dream without knowing all the steps from the beginning—Gerard was able to accomplish a lot in the three years since he started New Canadians TV from scratch: the TV show is broadcast all over Canada, the website has viewers from around the world...and it's still expanding!

✓ Introverts are patient and persistent

Without these qualities, Gerard wouldn't be able to make his dream of producing New Canadians TV a reality.

His persistence and patience, combined with networking and continuous learning helped him bounce back when he was feeling down.

√ Introverts seize a good opportunity

By using his intuition and keeping a meaningful objective in mind, Gerard was able to filter the opportunities for events and conferences that gave the best exposure and strategic networking. Through social media, he connects with people and organizations that are relevant to what he's currently doing and his plans for the future.

His *trick* of saying *"yes"* first, helps him to also benefit from the relevant speaking opportunities that come his way.

√ Introverts leverage their strengths

Gerard successfully leverages his introvert strengths. To name a few: *strategic thinking* (to realize his dream), *storytelling and media skills* (to make New Canadians TV a valuable project), *perseverance* (continues to strategically build his network), *proactivity* (always on the lookout for opportunities), *non-verbal communication* (uses social media to leverage his time and energy), *building genuine relationships* (builds trust), *business skills* (focused on what's relevant, juggling all aspects of producing a national TV show), etc.

√ Introverts appreciate integrity and value-based business

Working for a company focused more on making money than helping its clients, and not open to ideas that could serve both the business and clients…was not aligned with Gerard's values! The dissonance he felt while working for that immigrant-related website—feeling almost depressed in that work environment and reborn after stepping outside—influenced his decision to quit that job. A decision made with integrity.

His interest in balancing business with the social aspects of work led Gerard to build a business with integrity; making money while genuinely helping people.

√ Introverts have an acute awareness of their inner world

This ability was highlighted several times in Gerard's stories. He was aware of the difference between how others think about him and how he felt inside (*when others start seeing him as a success story*), or the stress associated with public speaking, or what's going on in his mind (*waiting too long to ask a question, doubting himself, then regretting not asking, etc.*).

√ Introverts are great at promoting a purpose-based business

They just don't call it *promotion*. :-) To Gerard, for example, it looks like a passion for making more newcomers aware of strategies that can help them succeed faster. While for those he interacts with to build his business, a willingness to make them aware of how they can make a more significant impact while growing their company or organization at the same time. It's all about re-naming, re-labeling, and hanging on that meaningful purpose that drives his business.

√ Time is an introvert's powerful resource

Since they need to balance their work with recharging time —to be more effective—introverts weave in the *time factor*. What do I mean by that? The breaks they take to recharge also helps them reconnect with themselves, so they can make better decisions, adjust if needed, and get more energy to achieve their dreams.

Gerard seems to master this resource, by gradually building relationships and trust in the services he offers, thus creating a strong foundation for his business. Or using his metaphor: he *plants good seeds in good soil* and has the patience to *reap the harvest*.

List of Introverts' Strengths
covered in this book
gabrielacasineanu.com/list-introverts-strengths

Chapter Five

CAROL

Sometimes—when things get too complicated—going back to the beginner's mind is always a better perspective.

— CAROL DONOHUE

Talking about complicated: if you find yourself getting overwhelmed by the technical details from Carol's stories…please hang on! We'll demystify them a bit along the way. :-)

I met Carol several years ago while I was in the process of starting the English-French Toastmasters Club, and was having a disagreement with an experienced member who was helping me start my club. We were having a difference of opinion over the best strategies to use (she is more conservative, while I prefer to think out-of-the-box). Getting frustrated, I reached out a higher-level member, which happened to be Carol. When we started talking, it was like a breath of fresh air! Carol quickly understood my ideas, and we co-organized a successful kick-off meeting.

She seemed to be so energetic, quick to answer my questions

and find solutions—all typically extrovert characteristics—I could never have guessed that she's actually…an introvert! I found out that she is one only recently when she answered my call for this book. Well, there was a clue that I didn't pay attention to: I usually don't get along so well with extroverts! :-)

I'll let you discover what helped Carol—a very anxious and nervous introvert—to become the confident person that I met; able to well articulate her thoughts and ideas even when she meets people for the first time.

Carol: I got a contract with a company because there was a team of 14 employees on the website and their manager wasn't working out. They went to HR, who agreed to give them a new manager. Well, that manager was worse than the first one! At that point they said: "Okay, we don't want to take a risk of this again, so let's ask for a contractor to be a project manager so we could have some interface." So they hired me. My manager was supposed to also be building a data warehouse that was going to go in with SAP [a business software program] implementation—but he didn't do anything. One day he said: "Now it's your responsibility!" So I went over to the organization and I asked: "Who is my counterpart to work with?" They said: "Well, we don't have a counterpart." So they sent me for SAP training, which was good. But then we also had a problem: we had a data warehouse and since the manager didn't do anything for six months— how are you going to get business requirements when six months of time was lost? That was a big challenge. Here's what I decided to do: as long as you have all the stakeholders in a room and all the decision makers, you can get something done. I'm a big believer in group work! So I brought about two dozen people in the room and started by saying: "We're going to create a data model." Everybody got scared and said: "This is IT, what do we know about IT?" I said: "No, no, it's really very simple. You have customers and you sell to your customers. And your customers have an address. What's the address?" Then somebody asked the question: "Do you mean the corporate address or the shipping address?" I said: "Ah ha, that's a very good point! We need to have a recurrence." So we started gathering this information and that information...and as it got on, it became like a fun game! People had their discussions of how they would want things done and they would hash it out then and there. Someone would think of an idea or somebody else would come up with an idea...so at the end of two whole days, the vice president said: "That's absolutely the best logical data model I've ever seen of SAP!" And I answered: "Well, thank you! That's the logical data model for my data warehouse. I'm happy to hear that it matches SAP and that this will be a successful project." The result was they were able to build the data warehouse they were looking for.

Gabriela: That was a great story!

Carol: Actually, I have another story to go with this. The purpose of building the data warehouse was to have full stream P&L [profit and loss] reporting because consultants in SAP said that you couldn't do the drill-down level of reporting within SAP. So I said: "Yes you can if you're smart and strategic about it." That's basically what I did too. They wanted to have profitability revealed so that you could drill down to a specific manager in the organization. They also wanted it to be by product, business unit, or market segment.

So it's like you're able to drill down and view it in different ways. This was in 1997, just at the beginning of different 3D images of data. What did I do? I took the chart of accounts and built the P&L statements and had the chart of accounts and the numbering order so that it would be in the correct cost element hierarchy grouping...so that it would just automatically flow out of SAP!

Gabriela: Carol, for those of us who are not familiar with these terms, can you explain a little bit what you just said? :-)

Carol: Alright! SAP is a software used by companies to store and correlate data from different departments and create reports. In this case, it was about the financial and controlling modules—so it was about accounting and financial reporting. In order to build a hierarchy, the hierarchy has to be such that things sum up in their bucket. So as long as it was logically in the order of the bucket—and the numbers are all for that item on the profit and loss statement—everything would roll up because it's in the hierarchy grouping. And then you could drill down, and you can keep drilling down as long as your hierarchy is logical like that. That was the other thing they needed to do on the SAP side so they had options for their reporting in both the data warehouse and the SAP. So it makes it better as a complete story.

Another example of overcoming a challenge was with Y2K. This was about the year 2000 approaching—the millennial code—when different programs had to be renovated and protected for when the changeover to the year 2000 came (because of the way programming was done with two-digit years rather than four digits). I was working with an insurance company at that point. What was interesting in the insurance business: one of their main programs needed to know the last Thursday of the month and the second Tuesday so they had their own homegrown program that did this.

Obviously, the first step was to renovate that program and make sure it worked in order to have a successful code renovation. But there was another issue to consider: as you are renovating code (and it took quite some time) you have to make sure that you're not breaking other programs when this program gives it data—so you need to have more renovations. The main question becomes: how to solve this problem in a way that is going to minimize any business disruptions?

What I did: I first identified each of the programs that needed renovations, who owned the data and who accessed the data. Then we built a database that identified everything we had, when we were going to renovate something, and what hooked into other programs in the data work.

The next thing that I did was to take the job scheduling for the whole month and see in which order the programs ran throughout the whole month. Then I put it into a Microsoft Project plan, gave a day's duration for each one of those programs. When I flipped it to network view, we could see the entire flow of data as it processed so we could renovate the code—the programs that were renovated were in order from the beginning, the first ones being processed all the way through to the end so that we got everything handled and made sure we renovated everything. That was a good challenge!

Gabriela: It was, even to follow what you're saying. :-) I have an IT background, so I can relate to what you're saying, but in my mind, I was like: how would some people understand that?

Carol: No, no, I know!

Gabriela: Actually I want people with this kind of knowledge to read this book as well.

Carol: What I did with the Microsoft Project plan is like using different tools to view things from different perspectives: you see the bigger picture, then you write it down to make sure people understand it…then find somebody who is not technical to read it. Here's another example: I wanted to learn how to ice skate backward. You can have people teach you this, but they might not use the right language. So I asked an eight-year-old: "how do you do that?" And she showed me!

Sometimes—when things get too complicated—going back to the beginner's mind is always a better perspective.

Let's talk now about another challenge, one of the most difficult so far: immigrating to Canada from the US. It's a long process, takes about a year (I think mine took 10 months actually). During this time, I had to wait in the country (Canada) and you're not allowed to work. So I had to keep myself busy. I joined Toastmasters, which is very good for public speaking and to build a network in my new home country. At one point, my husband said: "Why don't you take the time and write a book?" So that's what I did!

You know, it's one of those things: when life hands you lemons, you got to make lemonade! Every opportunity that you have is a choice you make—whether something is a stumbling block or it's a stepping stone! And I've had many such opportunities!

It was very difficult for me to find employment in Canada as an immigrant. But each time that I was out of work I wrote another book, like my second one: *Abdicate Down, Delegate Up?*

I used every opportunity from the time off to develop new skills and developing a Data Analytics as a Service (DAaaS) platform. So rather than looking at the challenge as the stumbling block of not having a job, I used my time wisely to develop other interests. That became a stepping stone to new avenues for career opportunities.

Gabriela: This means you're creative and resilient.

Carol: Well, it's like the saying *how to build a better mousetrap.* Create something better and people will come.

Gabriela: We introverts don't get knocked down so easily. If there's a challenge, we're like: "Okay. That's a challenge, what can I do from here?"

Carol: Any challenge is an opportunity.

Gabriela: True!

Carol: Let's talk now about Toastmasters. One of the things everybody says: "The fear of public speaking is greater than the fear of death." As an introvert, it can be hard. Public speaking was a challenge for me, which is one of the reasons that I joined Toastmasters. I still remember how in my second or third speech I lost my place. I got so rattled! But you continue with it and you work on it. How you get stronger is by working and improving your weaknesses. So it's continuous process improvement. Another thing about Toastmasters: it gets you the opportunity to learn from other people's perspective as to how you are perceived. That's beneficial too!

Gabriela: I'm curious, how did Toastmasters benefit you?

Carol: I don't get anxious or nervous anymore. I used to get very, very anxious and nervous. So just putting yourself out there and continually doing it helps!

Oh, I have a great thing I have to put in—by Ralph Waldo Emerson: "Sow a thought and you reap an action; sow an act and you reap a habit; sow a habit and you reap a character; sow a character and you reap a destiny."

So as you keep doing, it just makes your character stronger. Toastmasters is highly beneficial. It was very challenging though. As a Lieutenant Governor of Marketing, I was responsible for creating new clubs; I've created 20 and rescued five. One of the things that I did, I gave the exact same speech at every kickoff meeting that I organized. And I would have all the brand-new people, who wanted to become a Toastmaster, give me the feedback. By the time I got to the very last club, it was the best-polished speech that I've ever had!

So you know, it's like you take coal and you work hard enough...you get a diamond! It's the same type of thing.

Gabriela: So it does pay off to persist. Thank you!

I noticed some **introvert strengths** in Carol's stories, but I encourage you to check by yourself with the full **List of Introverts' Strengths** covered in this book:

gabrielacasineanu.com/list-introverts-strengths

√   **Introverts can find solutions to complex problems**

Carol was brought in as a contractor to solve complex problems and her managers recognized her contribution.

Introverts are capable of understanding complex systems, how different parts work together, what's missing...and to find creative solutions.

✓ Introverts recognize collaboration as an effective problem-solving tool

Being faced with a difficult situation—missing months of data—Carol looked for her counterpart to help her better understand the situation. But realizing there's none—and believing in group work—she brought together the stakeholders who might have some information available and made them collaborate to find the desired solution.

✓ Introverts are resilient: they don't back away from difficult challenges

Instead of backing off when she realized how challenging the situation was, Carol took on a leader's role and assumed responsibility for finding solutions. She gathered a team, addressed whatever concerns they had from the beginning, and made them work together toward the common goal: to create a database with information gathered from various sources so they can move forward. Her resilience helped in several situations.

✓ Introverts love the big picture

Adept at the concept *big picture first, details after*, Carol tried to see the situations from different angles first. That's another reason why she brought the stakeholders together and made them collaborate as a team. And to make it clear from the beginning, she started with what they're going to do *(the big picture),* which facilitated the process of gathering the required data from various sources. She was also able to keep the focus on the bigger picture throughout the session, so they didn't get lost in all those details—a strategic approach to problem-solving!

✓ Introverts are able to see things from different perspectives

When told they *can't do* something *(can't do drill-down level of reporting within SAP)*, Carol quickly analyzed the situation and suggested another perspective that facilitated the problem-solving process.

Introverts are also open to understanding other people's perspectives about them. Carol often asked for feedback while she was improving her skills as a Toastmasters member.

✓ Introverts are capable of explaining things in simple ways

Although they can understand and deal with complex concepts, introverts are willing to explain them in a simpler or different way when requested.

Due to time constraints, I asked Carol only once to do this during the interview. But she made herself available to explain in simpler terms if I ask again while revising her interview.

✓ Introverts think outside the box

Given the assignment to update a software program, Carol started by looking *outside*: she first identified all the connections and implications related to that specific program update, to minimize business disruptions. That helped her to identify what else needed to be done to successfully complete the original task: mapping the connections with other programs, (which would have been affected by or could have affected her program update), and creating a monthly time schedule (with priorities and task sequences required to successfully complete her assignment).

✓ Introverts' great work results build trust

Would you hire someone like Carol if you had a complex problem to solve? The complexity of the situations she talked about speak for themselves of the quality work she can do.

That's why introverts more often have to *share* the outcomes of their work (not about themselves), to build the trust needed to take their career to the next level. Of course, the *sharing* can be done in various ways, including non-spoken communication (via social media, for example).

✓ Introverts are good at using metaphors

Another non-traditional way to communicate a message! Carol used *how to build a better mousetrap* when she was talking about leveraging challenging times to create something more productive. Or *going back to the beginner's mind* when she talked about how to simplify complicated things—for example, she asked an eight-year-old to teach her how to ice skate backward.

✓ Introverts make great teachers

When she was not allowed to work, Carol turned to writing books to share her knowledge—a more suitable form of teaching for introverts.

Although Toastmasters improved her verbal communication, it was also a teaching opportunity for Carol—through her own speeches or the feedback she provided to other members.

So she was able to transfer her knowledge using different formats.

√ Introverts make the most of a situation

While she was out of work, Carol used her time in a productive way: she developed a *Data Analytics as a Service* (DAaaS) platform, wrote books, became a Toastmasters member and got involved in leadership roles. By doing these activities her anxiety decreased, she improved her verbal communication, boosted her leadership skills, and expanded her network.

√ Introverts like to motivate others

Carol shared several quotes that motivated her in challenging times, hoping they'll uplift us as well.

List of Introverts' Strengths
covered in this book
gabrielacasineanu.com/list-introverts-strengths

Chapter Six

CHARLES

I think it's really a trial and error; something that takes training, something that takes acceptance. But besides all these, there are some qualities that introverts exhibit that extroverts cannot have...

— CHARLES CHEN

Introverts are quite generous people and willing to help, especially if it's about a meaningful cause. So I wasn't surprised when—at the end of his interview *(see Chapter 2)*— Alex told me: "You have to interview Charles. He's very good at sales, but if you look at his LinkedIn profile picture he seems far away from the sales reps you might be used to!"

An introvert top sales performer?! That sparked my curiosity! After Alex introduced us, I had the chance to meet Charles via Zoom, and learn what helped him get these results in such a competitive field.

Later on, after Charles reviewed his interview transcript, he asked me to share this update with you...hoping it will inspire other introverts to become better at sales:

"We did the interview a day before my internal job interview. I got the job! I am the same person as before, but the job is more challenging and involves a lot of effort and strategic thinking. Also, I am one of the top performers on my team! :-)

Charles: I would start with the challenges of engaging in conversations with people that you are not very familiar with, you know, making small talk.

To help the company I work with, I often need to go to networking and social events where conversations usually start with small talk. So a lot of times I find myself not relatable to the people participating in the same event. I feel that they all have something to talk about—sports for example— and I am not relatable to the vast majority of the participants in such events. Or even about cues: when to start the conversation, from what point did I lose connection, and when to stop the conversation.

In a networking environment, I personally feel that a lot of these conversations are very superficial. There is no substance to it, it's just talking for the sake of talking. And sometimes I feel like carrying a conversation a little bit too long or too short. Or I run out of topics right away to continue the conversation. So that's one challenge.

The second challenge is having the confidence. I honestly think that—comparing myself to the majority of the sales-people who are extroverts—I do not appear to have the confidence of a typical sales rep. I tend to doubt myself first before believing in myself. I tend to see the negative outcome first before seeing the positive outcome. But I think I can turn that into a strength. Because when I anticipate a possible negative outcome, by not being confident, I put more work into it. You know, I put more preparation into, let's say, an interview. I put in more hours and practice more for that interview. Therefore, that makes me stand out and makes up for the lack of confidence from the start. And that is comparing to peers and colleagues at the same level in the company.

And the third challenge is about the sales cycle I have to manage. Again, this has to do with a lack of confidence. I feel that we, introverts, are more afraid of rejections—when customers and prospects reject you. I don't necessarily have a natural way of coming back and handling the objection, so I just tend to move on to the next one. However, there's a strength in that. Because we (introverts) don't have a huge amount of friends and people that would trust us in the sales circle, every time we connect with a stranger over the phone we tend to be more genuine. Because every new relationship, every new connection that comes into our personal or work life, we tend to treat it in a more genuine way and we tend to care more.

So I think these challenges often are turned into strengths by us, learning how to survive in a sales world dominated by people who are extremely confident, very sociable, who know how to network.

Gabriela: The first challenge you mentioned was about networking. How did you handle it?

Charles: In terms of networking, I try to start with people that I have seen before or met before, so I build up the confidence from there. And then, rather than stopping and leaving the meeting, I try to move on to the next person who is avail-

GABRIELA CASINEANU

able to talk. So I basically have to force myself into getting comfortable with having these small talks. Sometimes we might run into people who have a common interest or a common topic that we want to discuss further.

So you just have to force yourself, and hopefully, you run into another person that is also an introvert or someone who is also genuine. You got to put yourself through the situation because, if you feel uncomfortable and leave the event, then it's definitely not good for your brand. I feel that in sales, in any organization, your brand is just as important as your performance. You cannot have one without the other. I am a top performer in every company that I work with, but the brand is one thing. Managing myself as an introvert isn't something that I would say that I have completely solved as a problem. But it's something that I have developed over the years. Several years ago, when I got my first sales job I was extremely, extremely awkward, extremely stiff, extremely quiet and head-down, and didn't really do a lot of socializing.

But what made a little difference was learning to deal with and accept the fact that this is the real world. And I have to learn how to interact with people regardless of who they are.

Moving on to the next job, I was just lucky to have a couple of colleagues that were around the same age as me. We started talking and then, you know, you make friends with a few people. And naturally you make friends with 5, 10, 15… and you have a circle of trusted colleagues that you can communicate with. And then when it comes to socializing, when you know that there are a couple of colleagues in your vicinity (like if you go to a networking event and there's someone that you know at the event), that makes you feel more comfortable. And then it gives you a little bit more confidence because...hey, my colleague is there...my friend is there!

After I graduated, my first real sales job was in 2012. That's about six years ago. Again, I started as a very stiff and very awkward person, but now I'm someone who can perform really well. Today I am a much more confident person in terms of my ability to communicate: much more social with my colleagues, I am having way less challenges in starting conversations, and I'm building relationships with people that I work with.

However, I'm still an introvert: every time I finished working, every time I finish my job, I go home and I like to be by myself. I like to be left in peace, to be left alone.

Even today, if I have to go to social and networking events, my first instinct is to go like: *How can I not go? What valid reason can I come up with to not go to that event?*

But then I go because I have gotten so used to convincing myself and forcing myself to accept it. I got used to the environment of all the strangers looking at you, all the people that you're not familiar with, you know, I'm sharing in the same room with you in very close proximity...

I think it's really trial and error: something that takes training, something that takes acceptance. But besides all these, there are some qualities that introverts exhibit that extroverts cannot have, which is the ability to build that genuine connection fast!

And I'm proud of that. Because every time I have a conversation with someone, it can be a little bit more personal, a little bit more genuine. And you know, we can easily go into conversations about family and our stories, so it breaks down the barrier a little bit faster I think.

Gabriela: You covered a lot of interesting ideas! And it was funny: I had a question in mind—but didn't voice it—and you answered! Then I had another one, and you answered that one too.

Charles: I thought about this for a very long time. It's probably something that I've been aware of myself for the past few years. People like us, introverts, we like to talk. And we talk a lot when we find the person who is willing to listen.

Gabriela: That's true. You mentioned several times that it's hard work. Do you think it pays off?

Charles: I believe that hard work pays off for sure, 100 percent! When I was younger, I did not really understand the idea of working hard and working smart. And I felt that working hard is probably all you need. But, you know, as I've worked in sales for the past six years, I feel working hard is definitely a very good quality and something that you need to have in sales. But working smart is another thing. I'll give you an example: I work in payroll sales, right? So I work at ADP and we get credit when a customer processes their payroll with ADP. And I got this customer who signed up very recently and pays monthly payroll. So what that means is, for instance, for monthly payroll, if the contract value is worth $50—and is processed monthly—$50 times 12 is $600. Our fiscal year is ending in another two weeks and I'm quite close to making President's Club. So I thought about calling this monthly customer and say: "Hey, if it works for you, can you change your payroll frequency from monthly to semi-monthly?" The customer said: "Why would I do that?" I'm like: "Well, you know, if you want to help me out, I'm making

President's Club and I'm very close...but only if this works for your company. If it doesn't work, no worries, we'll still be friends. But if yes, that will be very, very helpful."

It just turned out that the customer had a conversation with his employees about getting paid semi-monthly rather than monthly. So in two days, the customer agreed to do semi-monthly and I doubled my revenue.

So it's a very small example of trying to be creative, trying to figure out different ways to get what you need without putting too much effort. Right? Because doubling the same amount of revenue, if I were to just 100 percent work hard but not work smart, it will probably take another day or two for me to get that revenue from somewhere else with a lot of effort. But with this, it only took one call. So I needed to think outside the box. I think people who think outside the box, people who are creative, are able to work smart as well. So in sales, working hard and working smart work hand-in-hand.

When you are desperate for sales, working hard definitely pays off. But when you want to go the extra mile, when you want to get that extra sale, then working smart will pay off.

Gabriela: I like how you said it!

Here's what I did with the other introverts that I interviewed: we had a discussion at the end about what introvert strengths I noticed being used to overcome their challenges. But you seem to be quite aware of your strengths. Do you want me to point out a few strengths that I've noticed in the examples that you gave?

Charles: That will be great! I think I know myself probably the best out of everyone else, but there's probably some things about me that I am sort of blind to. For instance, several years ago I didn't know that I am quite good at sales, right? I just gave it a try and I did well. And even today I still couldn't believe that I'm one of the top four performers in the country. I know it's part of my strength, but for someone who is very timid, someone who's very shy, very introverted, even until today I don't know how I did it. So if you could point me a couple of strengths that you noticed, it would help me to get more confidence.

Gabriela: The strengths I'll point out are based on your examples, but if you read books about introverts you'll find them there too.

First of all, you're perseverant when you want something. This is a big strength of introverts. Second, you mentioned several times that introverts are very good at making genuine connections. Because they're very good observers and they are caring, they can build great one-on-one relationships. That's why we don't feel okay in a big room full of people: not much time for meaningful one-on-one conversations. And introverts like to set meaningful objectives and have meaningful conversations (not small talk).

We are very creative as well. You thought out of the box to find solutions and overcome your challenges.

I like the fact that you're quite aware of where you are, but also I want you to recognize more of your inner strengths. Because I'm pretty sure you're confident about what you do well, even if the image that you project might not look as confident (like an extrovert would come across). You seem quite comfortable and confident in the way you handle the sales. So it might be the difference between how you feel about yourself and how others perceive you. But that doesn't mean that it's a weakness for you (how they perceive it). It might just be that you need to open up a little bit more so people see who you already are, what you can do, and what your strengths are.

If you didn't have confidence, you wouldn't have overcome those challenges and become a top performer. Don't expect yourself to be like an extrovert, because you'll never be one, and I don't think you need to be either. Like you're saying, introverts have a lot of strengths. We are strategic thinkers, we're very good project managers, we're great leaders and it's up to us to bring to the world all these skills and talents that we have. And you're doing very well!

You started at the beginning saying that you just wanted to try— and look where you are right now! And that's because of your strengths because you didn't give up. You tried to figure it out, to be creative, and find your own way through it.

And another thing: you recognize that one of the main differences between extroverts and introverts is how they get their energy. The extroverts get energized while talking to people, but the introverts need time by themselves to recharge their batteries. You already know that, and you're doing very well. That's why you were able to become a top performer in sales—because you were able to leverage, let's say, your extroverted behavior (when you are with others) with spending time by yourself to recharge. So you had a good balance in your life, which helped you get here. Makes sense?

Charles: I agree wholeheartedly. I actually have a job interview tomorrow—an internal job interview—and I'd like to incorporate into this interview some of the points that you mentioned. One of the interview topics that we will be covering is what I bring to this department. And I think that perseverance is a very good word. You have to be able to persevere through the difficult times in sales. Building one-on-one relationships is exactly what I was looking for. You know, I'm going into a sales role where I will have to be building relationships fast and make them prefer our ADP brand to others. If they have to like you first before they buy from you, that's going to be very useful.

And having meaningful conversations, I think that's a very important point. Because what I love about my job, aside from the money, aside from the recognition and all that, is having that meaningful conversation—that's the favorite part of any sales cycle that I have. Thank you for highlighting that.

Next is creative and strategic thinkers. I think I could be more strategic. We think a lot before we say something, we don't necessarily let emotions dictate what we do. I think that comes with some sort of maturity as well. But because we are introverts, because we are creative and anticipate several different possibilities before they happen…we try to think of different ways of handling them, sort of anticipating what's going to happen…

Gabriela: And that's strategic thinking: when you think in advance about what you need and start planning for it.

Charles: Yes, we're strategic!

Gabriela: You're also very good at research, which helps you come up with the right ideas, solutions, and information to help the client. Introverts are very good at research.

You're good at analyzing different situations, combining

concepts from different fields, from different experiences, so you have a lot of strengths to that you can bring to your new job.

Charles: Thank you. Wish me luck tomorrow.

Gabriela: Good luck! Anything else? Do you have any other questions?

Charles: I am good so far. Thank you so much for the conversation. I feel that I have learned a lot. It's good to talk to someone who knows people like me. Thank you!

Gabriela: My pleasure! Thank you, Charles!

Some of the introvert strengths I recognized in Charles' interview:

✓ Introverts are modest

"Even today I still couldn't believe that I'm one of the top four performers in the country," said Charles.

He also considers himself *lucky* for having colleagues the same age, but he forgets that a relationship—with someone the same age or not—develops with the participation of both sides. So he made a situation become his *luck*.

Why do I believe that modesty is a strength? It keeps us grounded and hungry to learn at any age, which is a must for self-growth and enjoying life more!

✓ Introverts aim to perform well in any profession they choose

Charles chose to work in sales and he became a top

performer in a field where extroverts are predominant. Which is remarkable because extroverts prefer speaking—as a communication style—getting energized by meeting and talking to people, which has exactly the opposite reaction for introverts!

As we can see from Charles' stories, when an introvert uses his strengths and makes sure he has enough time alone to recharge, he can outperform many extroverts at sales!

✓ Introverts are able to pinpoint specific challenges

Instead of saying something general—*I'm not good at networking*, for examples—Charles identified his specific challenges: *he doesn't relate to many topics that are usually used in small talk* and *when to start or stop a conversation*. Once he got specific, it became easier to find solutions that worked for him: he started with familiar people (his comfort zone) to build his confidence > moved to next person available to talk > and next…thus increasing his chances of finding a common topic or interest, or another introvert to talk to.

✓ Introverts can turn things around (find new perspectives)

Instead of letting himself get down by his *lack of confidence* (comparing with his peers) or the fear of rejection, Charles started thinking from a more positive perspective: *how he can use his strengths to become better at sales?* So he put more effort into planning a meeting with a client, researching and preparing for it, and practiced in advance. That made a difference!

To me, what he considered as a *lack of confidence* was more about knowing what works for him—as an introvert—instead of taking the extroverted approach for granted (that is the *right* approach to follow to get sales). Once Charles figured out what he needs, he had the confidence to use his approach, over and over again, and he became a top sales performer.

✓ Introverts are persistent and perseverant

Without having these strengths, Charles wouldn't have made it so far in a profession that demands so much energy. It works well for Charles because he gets motivated from the inside: he's willing to succeed in this field and feels rewarded by the quality of the relationships he builds in the sales process. Also, he honors his alone time (useful to recharge).

✓ Introverts easily notice what their priorities are

Charles realized that, in his field, the sales brand is more important than his performance. Instead of putting pressure on himself, Charles finds a way to motivate himself—which drives him out of his comfort zone and has a positive impact on his sales performance.

✓ Introverts learn to manage their strengths

Charles understood that it's a process to get to the level he wanted to be at! So he developed strategies that work for him.

He builds relationships with the colleagues whom he resonates with (easier for an introvert) and looks for his colleagues first at networking events. He realized that starting with something familiar will put him at ease and builds the courage to get out of his comfort zone. Then, using his genuine approach to make connections (another introvert strength), he's able to meet new people and build the trust that leads to sales.

✓ Introverts are open to self-development

That's what helped Charles transform himself from a stiff and *awkward* person (as he describes himself) into someone who performs very well, is more confident, more social, able to start conversations, and build relationships with colleagues and clients.

As fine observers of the inner and outer worlds, and social dynamics, introverts are open to self-development. Without these strengths, you can miss many opportunities that could possibly affect your life and career.

✓ Introverts are willing to force themselves when they want something

As Charles says, his first impulse is to not go to events. Then he finds a good reason to accept invitations and forces himself to go.

If you noticed, the reasons he uses are not related to the event itself, but to the possible outcomes: opportunities to get new leads, more sales, build more genuine relationships (what he actually likes about his job).

So the courage to force himself to go through an unwanted situation comes from connecting with a bigger, meaningful cause he resonates with. To him, *forcing* sometimes means *learning by trial and error*, other times, *accepting the situation,* (which is not easy either).

✓ Introverts find creative solutions (work smart not hard)

Being good observers of the inner and outer world, introverts learn a lot about themselves and the situations they go through. This helps them find creative solutions even while under pressure.

When Charles wanted to make the President's Club, he came up with a smarter way to reach his goal: he asked a client to switch the way he processes the payroll, instead of trying to make more sales, (which would take him more time, and probably would have missed the deadline).

✓ Introverts are keen to develop genuine relationships

Did you notice how Charles's handled the conversation with that client?

He was *honest* and shared the real *why* for his request—a *personal* reason, he wanted to achieve something. Also, he was *not attached to the outcome:* he reassured the client that the answer *won't affect their relationships.* And finally, he *patiently* awaited the client's answer *without putting extra pressure* on him.

All of these characteristics are appreciated in any relationship and have a positive, long-term effect.

✓ Introverts can leverage their strengths

By focusing on finding people with whom he can have meaningful conversations (instead of small talk), Charles filters out the situations where he can't use his strengths. This way, he leverages his energy, increasing the chances to find clients he can collaborate well with.

✓ Introverts use the introversion-extroversion differences as tools

Being aware of the main differences between extroverts and introverts—how they get energized, for example—helps

Charles navigate more effectively the professional landscape by finding solutions that work for him.

Instead of getting knocked down by the confidence projected by his peers, he looked at how he could counterbalance that with his strengths: anticipation, strategic planning, research, creativity, thinking before saying, and not allowing himself to get in the way…to name a few.

It also helps him design a better work-life balance that suits his personality.

List of Introverts' Strengths
covered in this book
gabrielacasineanu.com/list-introverts-strengths

Chapter Seven

LOUISA

I'll go out and be with people…then I'll find a quiet space and be by myself. I need time to process everything and just get back into my calm frame of mind.

— LM BAUMAN

I have a confession to make: while I was writing my first book, I was quite active in a Facebook group for authors. I shared what I knew and helped others—an introvert characteristic, right?—and I learned a ton about self-publishing from those who were more advanced than me. Yet, I rarely asked for something. At least not until I felt that I offered much more to that group! Does anyone else find it difficult to ask? :-)

LM Bauman is Louisa's pen name. We've met through that Facebook group and I'm glad that she answered my call for introverts to interview for this book. I didn't know much about her at that point, but I love how her stories complement the others' in this book!

She too had a problem asking for what she needs or wants! You'll find out what helped her overcome this and—even more important—what she discovered after! Plus...*I better let you read through!* :-)

Louisa: I have one big challenge. As an introvert, it's very hard to ask anybody for any help. You keep your troubles to yourself and don't bother anybody with it. I had been dealing with depression and had some marriage issues. I didn't really want to go to counseling; I didn't want anybody to know about it. I didn't think anybody would care or even believe my side of the story. But eventually, things got to the point where I reached out and finally got some help. I went to counselors and, surprisingly, my husband agreed to go with me. And I found out it wasn't as bad as I was afraid it would be!

Gabriela: Wow! What made you reach out? What was the trigger for you that you had to do this no matter what?

Louisa: Well, our family life was just getting worse and worse. We were unhappy, the children were unhappy...and I just thought: Well, this is no life for us! Nobody's having a good life and it's time to do something about it. I don't know what to do and I need help.

Gabriela: Do you remember if there was a specific moment that made you gather the courage to go out and reach out to other people?

Louisa: I might have been ready to go for marriage counseling sooner but I didn't think my husband would go with me. I had gone to my family doctor to get medication for the depression and she also recommended the counseling. But it was a long time before I was ready to do that. At one point, my husband and I had some kind of disagreement and I thought: Well this is it! Then I took courage in my hands and just asked him! It was just too hard trying to keep it all to myself, my problems...everything! And finally, one night at bedtime, I asked him if he would go with me to counseling. And I thought for sure he would say no and look at me like I was crazy. But he agreed to go. I was so glad that I finally asked for help and that I asked him to go with me! It really was worth it.

Gabriela: Great! Thank you so much for sharing this. It seems that you needed some time to process that idea, to get used to it, and at one point you reached out.

Louisa: Yeah, it took a long time and things got pretty bad before I was ready to ask for help.

Gabriela: Only to discover that it was better after that, right?

Louisa: Yes, definitely! I discovered that asking for help is actually a pretty good thing to do.

Gabriela: Did you ask for help more often after? So it became like a new habit for you?

Louisa: Yes, it did. I learned that it's truly not a terrible thing to ask for help. I was afraid of people. I thought maybe people wouldn't want to be bothered with me, or they would blame me for my situation. Then I found that they were happy to help, and the counselor was so kind and under-standing. They're so happy when they can do something for you, to help you out with your problems. And it's so much easier now that I started. Of course, when I decided to become an author, I had to ask for help all the time. I learned how to ask for help even in my family, to get their support.

Gabriela: Really great! I think many introverts will relate to what you said about not being willing to ask for help.

Do you have any other challenges to share, maybe from your childhood?

Louisa: Well. I came from a really big family. I'm the oldest of 13 children, so I rarely got the chance to be by myself. But I found ways to be by myself because I needed some peace and quiet to keep my sanity! So I would go up into my room and I would read. Or I would hide somewhere out in the orchard and read where nobody could find me.

Gabriela: I love what that you're saying: you found time for yourself because the need was so strong that you couldn't ignore it.

Louisa: Yeah, that's true. Sometimes my family would want to go on a picnic in the woods or something, and I would just rather stay home and read. It was too much—too much commotion!

Gabriela: I can imagine.

Louisa: Too much going on! I do enjoy being with people and I'm actually very friendly, but then afterward, I feel the need to just go and be by myself. I get overwhelmed. It's really important to me to find some space. I'll go out and be with people and have fun together. But then I'll find a quiet space and be by myself. I need time to process everything and just get back into my calm frame of mind.

Gabriela: Would you say that this became one of your main habits in life, which helped you in one way or another?

Louisa: To find time by myself?

Gabriela: Yes.

Louisa: Yes, this is very important. When I got married and had my own children, sometimes it was very hard to get some time to myself. But I always managed somehow, because it helped me deal better with life. I needed to be where it's quiet and nobody bothered me or made demands on me. I was just happier when I could find half an hour of alone time, or whatever I could manage.

Gabriela: It's good what you're saying because there are so many mothers who are introverts…and they don't find time for themselves. They think they just need to give, give, give… and at one point there's not much left to give because your energy is drained. I so love what you're saying, that you found time for yourself to recharge…because you felt that need. And you still feel it, you're still an introvert! We can't just take that "introvert coat" off of us, we have to deal with it.

Louisa: Absolutely. As much as I love people and see other people all the time, when my day is finally over, and the children are all in bed, it's time for just me. But then my husband will come in and he wants to spend time with me…sometimes it can be very hard to balance everything and keep everyone happy.

Gabriela: Oh yeah. I can understand that!

Louisa: When the children were small, they would take a nap in the afternoon, and I would have my peace and quiet time. I found it really a necessary thing for my sanity to have a little time for myself most days, to read, or sew, or do some scrapbooking.

Gabriela: I wish I knew that when my children were small! I didn't find time for myself and I was wondering why I'm so tired all the time. I thought that I had a health problem.

Louisa: Everyone takes mothers for granted way too much, and in the past, it was even worse. Nowadays, most people realize that mothers are people too and need some time for themselves. But in the past, a lot was expected of mothers. Like, they were expected to keep everyone else happy…to be all spiffed up when their husbands came home from work, with the house clean and tidy, the children happy, ready to serve him and make him comfortable because *he's worked so hard all day*. Now the expectations are not quite as high.

Gabriela: Nice. I think we have two great stories and they came with a lot of wisdom. I love how you presented them, weaving in the story of your introvert characteristics and how they help you to manage those difficult situations. Thank you so much for that.

Louisa: Well, you're welcome. I'm glad I could help you. You know, I thought: *I can give this a try and try to come up with something that will help you with your book...I don't need to hide myself away here!*

Gabriela: Thank you so much. I really appreciate it!

Louisa: I'm happy to help. I hope this will help other introverts overcome some of their challenges.

Gabriela: Yeah, that's the purpose of this book: to help other introverts who might not be aware of the things that we're talking about. I really appreciate that you were able to open up and share. I know that we introverts are kind of private people, we don't like to share too much about ourselves.

Louisa: That's so true. Glad I could help!

Gabriela: You really did! It was very good what you shared from a women's perspective, a mother's perspective, and a child's perspective in a big family...so you have many things in your stories. Thank you!

Some of the introvert strengths I recognized in Louisa's interview:

✓ Introverts are friendly people

Louisa admitted that she's very friendly, she likes to go out sometimes and have some fun. But she also noticed that she can't stay long; it becomes overwhelming after a while, so she needs to leave and be by herself to process everything.

It is the introvert's role to find the right balance between being with people and by themselves...so they can honor both their friendly side and their need to recharge, which is very important to deal with life.

✓ Introverts recognize their need for a quiet space

Whether they already know they're introverts or not, the need is so strong that cannot be ignored. It shows up as tiredness, both physical and mental.

Louisa realized from an early stage that she needs to find a quiet space for herself from time to time, to get back to her calm frame of mind. So she constantly looked for opportunities to meet this need throughout her life.

A note of caution though: there's also a downside of spending too much time by ourselves. It could become addictive, making us miss a deeper understanding of the outside world. There is a German proverb: *Don't throw the baby out with the bathwater.* There's a *real need* for introverts to be in a quiet space sometimes—to recharge or create, for example—but *staying away from people too much* is not a real need.

✓ Introverts don't like to bother or confront others

On one side—as a strength—these personality traits lead introverts to become more creative and resilient. Louisa found ways to spend time by herself, for example, even as a busy mom.

On the other side, the same trait could lead introverts to take on or accept far more than they would like to…thinking that they still can handle things. So they don't speak up or ask for help.

Louisa's marriage issues affected her health, leading to depression. Only when her emotional pain was too unbearable it triggered her to reach out and ask for help. Finding a meaningful reason (the well-being of her family) gave her the courage to break through her resistance and do something: she reached out to others for help.

✓ Introverts learn from their inner experiences

Introverts' ability to focus on their inner world allows them also to learn from their experiences, especially from those with the biggest emotional impact.

When Louisa realized the positive effect of asking for help, she started asking more often. It became easier in time, and she found ways to use this skill in other areas of her life (as an author, for example).

✓ Introverts like to help people

Their willingness to help others makes introverts great parents, friends, employees, teachers, psychologists, lawyers, social workers, writers, etc.

Which is a strength, right? Louisa is no exception. Although a very private person, she opened up hoping to help others through this interview—which shed light on some life aspects that were not covered in other interviews.

Yet, sometimes introverts need to remember that they are *people* too and that there are others out there who would like to help *them* as well (at least other introverts). So if we open up, asking for help could make them feel good...that they were able to help!

✓ Introverts take the time to get used to a new idea or situation

Anything new can be overwhelming for an introvert: our nervous systems are already too busy to absorb a lot of information and emotions all at once!

Why do I consider *taking time* as a strength? It allows introverts to weight the pros and cons, and get used to a new idea or situation. By spacing out a large amount of information, it becomes easier to *digest it*. It also gives them more time to reflect so they can sort out if it looks like a good opportunity or not.

True to her introverted nature, Louisa took the time to get used to the idea of asking for help. That allowed her to find a good reason for pushing herself out of the (painful) comfort zone, and to build up the courage to seek help.

If you're not used to the concept of a *comfort zone*: in coaching, we call this a situation one is familiar with. It may or may not be comfortable to stay in that situation. For Louisa: not asking for help when she was in that stressful situation was her *comfort zone* (she was familiar with the situation, even if she didn't feel comfortable being in it).

✓ Introverts find creative ways for spending their quiet time

There are many ways introverts can spend their quiet time, which is so important to keeping their sanity.

We've got some good examples from Louisa: she spends her quiet time reflecting, in nature, reading, sewing, or scrap-booking.

List of Introverts' Strengths
covered in this book
gabrielacasineanu.com/list-introverts-strengths

Chapter Eight

ADINA

Find the right tool to express yourself— that bridge! Because the tool is the bridge between you and the project or the thing you want to do... (or the person you want to talk to).

— ADINA ANA VOMISESCU

There are several of us featured in this book who changed their career direction. But if you find it strange that three of us—Mihaela, Adina, and I—started in engineering...well, there is a reason! Although we met in Canada for the first time, we're all Romanian-Canadians. But when we started our professional paths in Romania, almost all of the roads led to...engineering! :-) Some people went into medicine and law...but there was no option to obtain a psychology degree.

I went to a high school that focused on math and physics, but I bought a psychology manual in the last year...something in me was curious about that topic! No wonder why I'm now passionate about...introversion! :-)

So if you're one of those introverts who wonder what to

focus on, you might be surprised that one place to start looking is at those signs you got in your early years (things that resonated with you, the moments you remember vividly, the topics you were really interested in…)

I'll let you now discover Adina's challenges along her path.

Adina: My biggest challenge seems social but it touches both the professional and personal. So it's a bubble that covers everything.

Gabriela: What was it about?

Adina: I feel very uncomfortable to be put on the spot.

Gabriela: What do you mean by *put on the spot*?

Adina: To be the highlight of the day or the group. I like to be part of a group, or an event, or a situation, but I don't like to be the highlight. For example, if it's a situation in which I can help, I will jump in to help, but somehow from behind. I'm not gonna say come and follow me. That's the biggest challenge, I think because sometimes you have to step in and do something or interact. I'm interacting but very cautiously.

Gabriela: What do you mean by very cautiously?

Adina: I'm always thinking before: how will I affect the situation? I feel that it doesn't matter if the help comes from me or others. Maybe because I'm shy, I don't want them to say: "It's Adina who did that."

That's how I've always been. If you gave me a credit, I always shy away from it.

Gabriela: Where is this coming from? Is it hard to accept the acknowledgment?

Adina: That's a hard question. *Why do I like to act like a shadow?* I don't know why.

Gabriela: You don't have to go into the "why." I'm talking about acknowledgments: if someone gives you credit, you don't feel comfortable. That's what you said?

Adina: Not that I don't feel comfortable. I'm okay with it, but I don't make a big fuss about it.

Gabriela: So why do you consider it a challenge?

Adina: Because I live in a world that collects credits. I see that the more credits you have, no matter if they are genuine or not, you kind of advance more or faster.

Gabriela: So do you consider that it is fake?

Adina: Yes, sometimes. That's another challenge: I see in the world lots of fake situations. Which sometimes I agree with, sometimes I don't. Maybe that's a fear or maybe I don't like to be fake, I don't know.

Gabriela: This book is about how you overcame your biggest challenges. So what helped you to overcome this challenge? Or were you able to overcome it?

Adina: Yeah. I always fight with myself. And art helped me a lot to overcome this.

Gabriela: In what way?

Adina: Because it's a way of communication with people and it's more genuine.

Gabriela: Is it because it doesn't require words? It's a different form of expression.

Adina: Probably, that's one thing. It gives me a voice.

Gabriela: A way to express yourself?

Adina: Yeah. It gives me a voice and it's a tool that I use. Instead of putting myself out there, it's the art that talks. So it's like a mask maybe—I don't know. It's not me, it's the *art*.

Gabriela: Oh, interesting. Would you say that, because of that, you are able to be out there? Because you're kind of promoting and talking about your art, it's not about you.

Adina: Yes. It's about art in general—even if I talk about a piece of art that I did—I don't talk about myself. I talk about the process, the engagement, the message. Again, I don't want to put myself on the spot: it's the art, not me!

Gabriela: I saw you at the opening event of an art exhibition. You were all out there, talking to people. I'm shyer than you in those situations. So what help you do that? How did you get there if you were not like this from the beginning?

Adina: It was actually very hard at the beginning because I considered that I can't talk about my art. But slowly, slowly I learned to talk about the art but not from a personal point of view. I consider it a tool that helps communication. So whether it's the art I created or the art was created by somebody else, it makes me comfortable to talk about it—maybe to express feelings that otherwise I wouldn't be able to express. Whatever is frozen in me, I can get it out when we talk about art.

Gabriela: Wow. That's really interesting.

Adina: Yeah, that helped! The process was okay, but it was slow. At the beginning it was hard, let's say 20 years ago when I started to go out with my art (because I created it all my life). But somehow, I found this way to get it out there and eliminate the personal—which always had been in my way.

Gabriela: That's really interesting.

Adina: And now I see that we're all artists. Some are writers, some are musicians...art is universal! So this is a universal language and I feel comfortable with universal language.

Gabriela: I love it!

You said it was a challenge all your life. Where are you right now? Would you say that because you find this universal language, this tool, you are more comfortable to be out there?

Adina: Yeah, I am more comfortable. For example, to explain how difficult it was for me: you know, as an artist you have to have your own show. I always prefer to be part of a group show. When I had my own shows, it was very, very hard for me. I have to be the one on the spot. I have to be the highlight of the evening. But because I found this universal language, I don't consider my art as my own. I consider it an expression of the universal consciousness. So I consider it as a tool. I'm using it as a tool.

Gabriela: Would you say that you're the conduit; the channel through which the universal consciousness expresses itself? That's what you're saying?

Adina: Yeah, that's what I'm searching through art. I don't know if I'm there yet. I'm still searching, but the search is very beautiful.

Gabriela: Yeah, the process of searching—in itself—is very beautiful. I have a question for you because I'm an artist as well. I noticed that, for me, if I just need to create a piece of art and put it in a group exhibition, I don't like it as much as when I create a body of work for a solo exhibition—where the different artworks are connected through a common thread. For example, in a solo photo exhibition, I took people on an emotional journey, where they go from one photograph to another. I found that I can express myself better in a project like that than in an individual piece of art that is part of a group exhibition, which puts together artworks that don't have much in common. Where are you with this?

Adina: Every group exhibition is a nice challenge. It makes me think where I am in that theme, in that environment. It's not a challenge for me to be part of that group exhibition. I can always create artwork or, if I use something that is already created, I can adjust it to the theme of that group exhibition.

Gabriela: So you still want to find a link between your piece and the other pieces. You don't just throw one piece in and that's it.

Adina: No, no. I find the link, always.

Gabriela: Nice.

Would you like to continue to talk about this? Or about another challenge that was quite difficult but you were able to overcome?

Adina: Yeah. I had to fight with myself because I do realize that I'm too shy. And it's difficult sometimes to be in the background. I realized at some point that it makes life very difficult to just stay in a corner because you want to be part of something.

Gabriela: What helped you overcome that?

Adina: I pushed myself. My subconscious, my inner voice said that you have to be part of this world. You can't live isolated. I like to stay in nature by myself and just be friends with trees and flowers and animals. I'm very, very comfortable with them. But I love people too. And people communicate, so I realize that I have to do that too.

Gabriela: You have to find a way to do that too. That's what you're saying?

Adina: Yeah. But I don't resist too long, I need to recharge in my own space. Sometimes I'm going to exhibitions, and it's uncomfortable because you go, and you don't know anybody, and you have to try to find a way to communicate. I can do it, but not for long.

Gabriela: I totally understand. That's totally an introvert thing. My question is: how do you find a way to communicate? You said you go to exhibitions where you don't know anyone. How do you approach someone? How do you start a conversation?

Adina: I try to talk about what was created, which I'm genuinely interested in. So I'm interested in the process of creation and the pieces that are out there. I'm interested in the process of creation and how people connect themselves with the world, with the universe. It's an ongoing interest.

Gabriela: So what I'm hearing: you actually put your shyness aside and you tap into your curiosity…

Adina: Yeah.

Gabriela: …to find out more about what you're interested in, about these meaningful things that you're curious about. And that helps you make that connection and start the conversation?

Adina: Yes. That's what helps me.

Gabriela: It's good because you immerse yourself in art, in the universal language that you're comfortable with. And from there you get curious (because you're curious about this topic), and it just flows from there. That's what I'm hearing.

Adina: Yeah, that's exactly what I do. Sometimes I go and just look. If I don't feel like talking I just have an inner dialogue with the art or the environment. Because I like all sorts of events, not only visual arts. I like poetry, music, writing, drama…everything that is about how people create. And how they feel on this journey.

Gabriela: Are you also interested in the impact the art has?

Adina: Oh yeah, I'm very interested. Especially lately, I'm very interested in two directions: one is how art helps people with disabilities or mental issues to find themselves, the other is how we affect the environment through art.

Gabriela: So would you say that you're interested in meaningful topics related to creativity? In the impact of creativity in different shapes and forms, in different environments, the natural environment or mental health environment?

Adina: Yes.

QUIET LESSONS FOR THE INTROVERT'S SOUL

Gabriela: That's interesting.

Okay, so we talked about your shyness and that you don't like to be in the spotlight. I love the idea that you felt—at one point—that you have to be part of this world. So you started to push yourself in that direction.

We talked about art as a tool—as a universal tool. And about the meaningful projects you're interested in right now. Is there another challenge that you had to face and were able to overcome?

Adina: It's always the social, that's the big bubble. Social challenges on a professional level. I'm a Montessori teacher as well, and I found that the Montessori philosophy also addresses this issue of how we find ourselves and how we integrate ourselves in this world. It starts from an early age, from childhood. Dr. Maria Montessori is very focused on individuality, how to help each child express himself/herself. How to find that voice of being there. So as teachers we look at the individual, not necessarily at what we have to teach each day. Of course, we have a lesson plan but we try to include each child with his or her way of expression.

Gabriela: What is the challenge here? You said that is a professional challenge.

Adina: The challenge, again, is that you have to put yourself on the spot. You are the teacher. You are the one that has to be followed.

Gabriela: As an authority?

Adina: This is the challenge because I don't see the importance of authority. My whole idea is we're all together. We're all unique, but we are together. We have to accept each other, each other's uniqueness, and work with that. This method helped me to handle this situation, so it was actually helpful in my own personal life.

Gabriela: Would you say that you're more of a facilitator than a leader? Maybe that's why you don't like to be in the spotlight because you're a facilitator. You like to facilitate something to happen, while the leader is someone who is in the spotlight and says: "Follow me!" leading toward something. And you actually want to facilitate something to happen. That's what you're saying?

Adina: Exactly, you touched the spot!

Gabriela: I totally recognize myself in what you're saying, I'm just using my words.

Adina: You touched the spot again, that's what it is!

Gabriela: I'm a professional coach and when people say: "You're the expert," I'm like: "I'm not the expert. I'm just facilitating the clients' change, helping them to figure out what they need." I don't like to give advice. Even if I might know more on certain topics, I invite them to explore other perspectives (based on what I know)… so they open their mind, thus broadening their awareness. Then I'll let them figure out which option suits them and the situation better. And in the process, sometimes they discover other perspectives as well. So I bring a facilitation approach, helping something to happen. Even for my workshops: I always choose a topic I'm interested in and weave in the facilitation approach. That's why I'm comfortable leading these workshops because my purpose is not just to provide information, but to create a mind shift that leads to transformation in one way or another. I'm okay with people considering me a workshop leader because this way they'll open up to see what they can learn—and that helps my facilitation to have a bigger impact. Even if I'm doing a presentation, I talk about different perspectives to help them light up different parts of their brain so they can make new connections before figuring out what they want.

Adina: I see the point. I do workshops as well, and that's that point: I see myself as a facilitator, not somebody who directs you.

Gabriela: Introverts like to collaborate, and this is another way to collaborate with participants…instead of leading them.

Adina: Yeah. Collaboration is something that I really like.

Gabriela: Nice. When did you start being a Montessori teacher? That's what you did from the beginning of your professional career? Or there was something else first?

Adina: I became a Montessori teacher once I had my kids. Through my daughter, I came into contact with the Montessori school because she went to a Montessori preschool. And I was fascinated by this method! Then I started looking into it, and I did my Montessori training (about 23 years ago). Prior to that, I was an artist and I started as an engineer. But I didn't want to continue on that path.

Gabriela: That's what I wanted to hear. :-) I have my professional journey as well. I started as an engineer, then changed to other fields: coaching, art, writing…

I wanted to check with you because I want to see if you're also on a kind of a search for your soul. Would you say that you're trying to see where you fit better, what resonates with you more?

I had no regrets switching from engineering to something else (coaching). And through that, my creativity increased, and I've started expressing myself in art. I didn't stop myself by thinking that I'm not formally trained in art. Or that English is my second language, I just launched myself into writing books. So I'm looking at life like a journey of self-discovery. Is it something that you're looking for as well?

Adina: To me, it's not self-discovery, but maybe self-expression. Of course, you discover yourself in the process. But, I don't know, something makes me uncomfortable when I say *self*. Again, it's going back to that thing: if I say "self" it's too individual, too egotistic. I don't know why I think that because we're all *self*.

Gabriela: Do you consider *self* as something isolated?

Adina: Yes.

Gabriela: Because to me, it's something different. You know, you talked about universal consciousness. To me, the *self* is just one of the expressions of the universal consciousness. So I don't see it like something separated, isolated. I'm just trying to understand if it's about labeling here, and we're saying the same thing or we're saying something different. So for me, when I say *self-expression*, it's more from a perspective of *I'm one of the ways the universe is expressing itself*. And I continually work on understanding and expressing myself, to see what else is there: what other strengths and skills I have, what else I can create... So I'm in this quest of discovering things, instead of just getting stuck in *I'm an engineer and I'll retire from that*. So that's where I'm coming from with my question.

Adina: Now that we're talking—and this is my personal perception—maybe it's because I'm seeing this *self* as exclusive. And I'm always about inclusiveness. Which gives me the courage to go out there and—like you said—talk to people that I don't know. It's about inclusion. I forget about *self* when I talk to them. I embrace this tool of art, and art is very inclusive! So I'm not talking about *self* (myself), I'm talking about a process that includes me and the others as well (even if they're not artists). Art includes, whatever form of art it is.

Gabriela: Would you say that's giving you a sense of belonging, the self in the bigger picture. You said inclusiveness.

Adina: Yeah. Inclusiveness, not only myself but everybody: universal inclusiveness, in which we are all unique. And, as you said, we have a *self*. So in a way, in order to be inclusive, I set my own self apart. That gives me courage!

Gabriela: Do you consider *self* as the *ego*?

Adina: Yes. The way it goes now in the world, it's an *ego*.

Gabriela: So that's what you put aside. You put your *ego* aside when you go out there to find that inclusiveness, and that connection.

Adina: Mine and the others' *ego*. Because *ego* is something that frightens me. That's true. Sometimes I can see *egos* very well. That's a big problem. I can see *egos*.

Gabriela: That's interesting. How do you see *egos*?

Adina: I read about them, I hear them, I see them…

Gabriela: So you have like a lightbulb that lights up when you notice an *ego*?

Adina: Yeah. And that frightens me, that creates separation. In other words, I would like this whole world to be about inclusiveness. And *ego* creates exclusiveness. It creates exclusiveness, a disconnection even within us (ourselves).

So maybe that's why I put aside the *ego*. And I try not to see the *egos* (other *egos*) when I talk.

Gabriela: So you want to connect with…

Adina: …with something more profound that is in us. Because we all have that.

Gabriela: Would you say that the *ego* is the opposite of being genuine and authentic?

Adina: Yeah.

Gabriela: And you like to connect with that authenticity.

Adina: Yes, I like to connect with something that is authentic and real. Because that's how we live our life now. We live our life with ourselves. *Ego* stays in the way of connection and authenticity.

Gabriela: Nice. Anything else you would like to add?

Adina: I would like to say that, as much as social media is criticized now, it does help introverts!

Gabriela: I totally agree! I'm living proof of that.

Adina: Yes, there are glitches here and there with social media but it does help.

Gabriela: In what way does it help you?

Adina: In the communication field. Because sometimes I find it easier to just interact on social media.

Gabriela: Yeah, me too. I'm interacting on social media more because I have the laptop screen between me and those people. :-) Also, I can go there whenever I want so I can control my time for interaction. Sometimes I don't feel the need to interact, so I don't go there. But when I feel the need to socialize and there's no one around, social media helps me.

Adina: Yeah.

Gabriela: There's another way that social media helped me. When I started my coaching business, I started using social media more, sharing information, commenting, engaging in discussions... As an introvert, I don't like to talk about myself. But when I started doing it, I realized there was nothing wrong with that. On the contrary, people were connecting with me at another level when I said something about myself. So social media helped me a become more open with others. It's another way of exploring the world but in a safe way, because you control what and how much you put out there...kind of like taking baby steps. It's also helping to see yourself through the eyes of others.

Adina: Again, social media is a tool.

Gabriela: Yeah, exactly. It could also become an addiction.

Adina: Oh yeah, that too. We have to be careful with that. But if you create, it won't become an addiction. You have your creation field too.

Social media also helped me to understand myself otherwise I wouldn't have realized that I don't like to be on the spot. Because sometimes on your own page you have to put yourself there, to say something about yourself. This is how I found out that I'm struggling with this. But it helps because it's a tool. I'm still watching, I'm very careful with what I put up there. I'm trying not to put personal things. Most of the time I put my art and I have to say something about it. So it's good and, at the same time, it's challenging.

Gabriela: Did you find that it gets easier in time?

Adina: Yeah, definitely.

Gabriela: What I found about myself: I can express my feelings much easier on social media than in front of people in real life. If I just saw something and I'm happy, I can say that on social media. If I'm with someone else I might not, I might still have a very serious face while I'm happy inside.

Adina: I did a course in clowning just because my youngest son has a tendency to be a clown —he has a very happy, bubbling personality—and I wanted to learn how to communicate more with him. Just putting that red nose on my nose, it was so liberating! I found that: "Oh, I can say anything! I can do anything!" Of course, things that won't hurt people or the situation.

Gabriela: It gave you permission?

Adina: It's like a mask you put on and you can be yourself.

Gabriela: Hmmm…that's very interesting! It's like a mask that actually allows you to be yourself.

Adina: Yeah.

Gabriela: That's really cool! I love it. It's interesting how— for introverts—you need that tool to communicate.

Adina: Yeah, I would say as an introvert I really needed to find that tool to communicate. So whether I found it in art or in the clown nose, or in social media…I always use a tool.

Gabriela: Really nice. Would you say that it's also helping your personal life? You don't have to go into details. I'm just curious. When you start expressing yourself through these tools, would you say that it's improving your personal life as well?

Adina: Yes, definitely. It helps a lot.

Gabriela: Going back to what you were saying earlier: it doesn't make you feel isolated anymore?

Adina: Right.

Gabriela: It gives you some tools to connect…

Adina: I find that using a tool always helps to communicate with people, whether they are your immediate family or people that you don't know.

Gabriela: Nice. You talked about some interesting tools to help introverts understand not only how they are, but also how to bridge the gap between "I want to connect" and "I don't know how." It's really powerful.

Adina: For example, thinking about interviews: if I find the tool, it's not difficult to go to an interview.

Gabriela: What kind of tool would you use for an interview?

Adina: Well, it depends on the situation. Let's say you want to engage in a project. Maybe you think "I'm not that strong in that field. I need to prepare myself more before I join that project, or to go for the interview for that project." You can wait your whole life to become an expert.

Gabriela: And you're still not an expert at the end of your life. :-)

Adina: Yeah, exactly. If you can find a bridge, something that you really like about the project—again find the tool—you start with that. Because on the way, you can become more professional: you can do more research…and you can be open for anything. But if I block myself saying: *Okay, I'm not an expert in this field, I will not even start.* And maybe you'll find that you actually know more than you think, and you have expertise in that field. It's again, finding the tool.

Gabriela: Cool. That could be the topic or the title of your chapter title in this book.

Adina: Yeah. Finding the right tool to express yourself—that bridge! Because the tool is the bridge between you and the project or the thing you want to do…

Gabriela: …or the person you want to talk to…

Adina: Yeah. As you see, it goes back again to not putting yourself on the spot…but finding the tools to communicate what you have in your mind, what you want to express or do, what you want to create!

Gabriela: Nice. I think we have a lot.

Adina: I want to add something: It took me years to realize and accept that I'm an introvert. And once I accepted, somehow life became easier.

I took a personality quiz and it came out that I'm the most introverted in my family. And surprisingly, my kids said: "You're not an introvert. How can you say that?" So that played in my mind: *You're not an introvert!* But I had the quiz results to show them.

Gabriela: Being an introvert doesn't mean you cannot come across as an extrovert. Especially if you feel comfortable with the person you're with, and it's a conversation that you like. You're totally normal. But you cannot talk forever because your energy gets drained, and you still need time to recharge—that's specific to introverts. It's not about if we can talk or not. There are a lot of misconceptions about that.

Adina: Yeah. Because they know me, I stand up for things that I consider meaningful, things I consider right!

Gabriela: That's exactly what introverts do: they stand up for things they consider meaningful (which actually give them the energy to stand up). You're able to put yourself aside and just stand up for that you believe in.

Adina: Yes. And another thing I like is equity. I'm always looking for equity in any situation, any issues. So when it comes to equity, I forget that I'm an introvert! Actually, if I go back, equity is number one in my life. Whether it's social or...especially now what's happening with the environment. Because we have to live in equity. That's why—for me— equity is number one.

Gabriela: You say equity is number one. We already talked about inclusion and that we're all one. I think they're all related.

Adina: Yeah, exactly.

Gabriela: You cannot say "we're all one," if you don't think about equity, about inclusion (not exclusion)...and these kinds of things tie in very well.

Adina: And it's not only about people. It's in the natural world too, which now suffers a lot because of inequity.

Gabriela: Because of humans. Because nature doesn't have inequity.

Adina: Because of *ego*!

Gabriela: Humanity's *ego*.

You said you suffer. I'm kind of looking forward because I know that nature cannot handle mistreatment forever. It will start taking its rights, so I trust that things will be okay. Maybe nature will help that *ego* in humans to wake up and understand what's happening. So maybe this ecosystem—which includes humans and nature— might have a way to kind of regulating itself to be okay. And if one part doesn't play well with this equity, the other part (nature) might shake it somehow.

Adina: In the *ego*. :-)

Gabriela: Yeah. Because I see a lot of things happening in the natural world these days. Those big waves, tornados, earthquakes… That's nature asking for its part, for equity, for harmony. So I trust the future, I'm not fearing. I see what's happening as part of a bigger picture of finding that balance, finding that harmony.

Adina: Yes, we have to live in harmony.

Gabriela: Yep, we're getting there: slowly but surely. :-) That's how I see it.

Adina: We will have to invent the tool for equity. That's a very interesting journey, to find that tool that will bring equity and balance between us and the natural world.

Gabriela: I'm not sure if there's only one tool.

Adina: Yes, I think there are more.

Gabriela: And we're working, humanity is working on that. It's an evolution.

Adina: I agree, it's an evolution.

Gabriela: That's why I'm saying that it's a self-discovery journey, for humanity as well: how to live in harmony with the whole world!

———

Some of the introvert strengths I noticed in Adina's interview:

✓ Introverts are okay being helpful without being in the spotlight

Adina mentioned this several times: she's motivated by and wants to help the causes she cares about, but she doesn't look for *credit*.

Being in the spotlight adds extra pressure on the already sensitive nervous system of the introvert. Feeling that all eyes are on you adds to the overwhelming input received from the outside world (we're very fine observers), making it difficult to be yourself.

Why is this a strength? Because, by eliminating the extra pressure caused by being in the spotlight, introverts can rely on another strength: focusing intensively on what they're doing. This allows their brain to perform better, leading to more valuable outcomes.

✓ Introverts interact cautiously: they think before they act

While visiting an art exhibition, for example, Adina starts by reflecting on an art piece. Becoming curious about the creative process or the meaning of that artwork, she then finds a meaningful starting point to initiate a conversation.

This seems to be a useful way to get over the introvert's block: *What should I say?* By interacting cautiously, you're prone to make fewer mistakes and find better ideas to exchange with the others.

I'm aware that some people might not consider this an introvert strength. They might notice a brief delay in responding and quickly label it as *slow thinking* or *lack of ideas*. But if you were able to take a snapshot of all the ideas that cross the introvert's mind during that brief delay, you would be amazed by the amount of thinking that happens during that time.

✓ Introverts are truthful and can spot fake compliments

That's one of the reasons Alina doesn't like to accumulate *credit*! She is very aware that she lives in a society where *credit* is considered valuable. But she also noticed that some people exploit the system, leading to fake credit.

Since introverts are very good observers of human behavior and social interactions (it's like a *sixth* sense), they can easily spot fake compliments. Their unwillingness to make a fake compliment helps them to build more genuine relationships.

✓ Introverts find creative ways of expression and communication

Adina found that *art* is a great communication *tool* for her, allowing both self-expression and a way out of her *comfort zone* (to fulfill her need to communicate with others). She uses art as a genuine way to communicate, like a universal language that she can tap into—which also helps keep the ego at bay.

Wearing a red clown nose is another *tool* that Alina finds useful and liberating. It allows free expression, giving her permission to be herself.

✓ Introverts don't easily give up

Adina felt compelled to honor her inner calling: to reach out to people, to express herself, and to deliver meaningful messages about the causes she deeply cares about (people with disabilities and protecting the environment). Driven by what's important to her, she found ways to break through her inner resistance and get out of her comfort zone (being by herself or in nature, for example).

She found that putting on a *mask* (letting the *art* speak, not *her)* and using art as a *communication tool* makes it easier to break through her own resistance.

Once she was able to find a *tool,* communication became easier and even enjoyable because she could take herself out of the process. This is what introverts usually want: to deflect the attention from them to something else (which they consider more important).

✓ Introverts put themselves in a larger context

Adina considers her art—in its various forms—a universal language. And she's comfortable with such *language.* It makes her feel that she's part of something beautiful, bigger than herself, that's being expressed through her, continuing to search and unfold…a process she really enjoys.

One of her main values being equity leads Adina to explore and support bigger causes (disabilities/mental illness and protecting the environment) through the medium (*tool*) of her choice (*art*).

✓ Introverts feel the need to connect with others

That's what drives Adina to push forward, to not stay back. Her inner voice told her that she has to be part of this world, so isolation is not a solution—just a temporary state to recharge in her own space, before returning to contribute to building a better world through the causes she deeply cares about.

✓ Introverts get creative when they want something

Very intuitive and attuned to her inner wisdom, Adina found ways to put her shyness aside when she wants to start a conversation. Immersing herself in an environment that makes her feel comfortable makes it easier to spark interesting conversations and from there... she goes with the flow.

So she intentionally chooses the environments that work for her.

✓ Introverts are comfortable with their inner dialog

Why is this a strength? First of all, it's a great idea generator!

Also, by allowing the inner dialog to occur without the pressure of having something to say, introverts can be part of the outside world without interacting with it. Combined with their ability to take in many details, the inner dialog could improve their perception of the world.

For Adina, this happens at some exhibitions she attends: when she can't find an *ice-breaker* to initiate a conversation, she enjoys her inner dialog with the art or the ideas that the artwork has triggered in her mind.

✓ Introverts make great facilitators

Many introverts characteristics are key to becoming a great facilitator: a willingness to contribute to others development without being blinded by your ego, fine observers of the human behavior and social interactions, ability to notice the atmosphere and the subtle shifts within it, good connection with intuition, strategic thinking (preventing negative behavior to affect the learning environment), ability to adapt to various learning styles and situations, focus on facilitating growth instead of sharing information.

Yet, these characteristics become more powerful when introverts focus on topics they found meaningful.

Adina loves being a Montessori teacher. And she became one after she realized how much she resonates with the Montessori method of education, which is aligned with her own beliefs.

✓ Social media is a great communication tool for introverts

Do you wonder why I consider this an introvert strength?

Because it's a powerful non-spoken communication tool, which suits better the introverts' style than spoken communication! You can switch it on or off at your convenience. And it's an additional way to fine-tune your observations about both your inner and outer worlds.

Adina noticed it too: social media is a powerful tool for the introverts who are willing to embrace it! It improved her personal life by making her feel less isolated and more connected (even with family). It became a more genuine marketing tool for her, an easier way to stay connected and communicate without the feeling that she's put on the spot. It's also a self-growth tool (to increase self-awareness and overcome some of her inner barriers), and a way for self-expression…which helped others to become more aware of her talent. And the best part: she's able to protect her personal life!

What do you think: would the world benefit if more introverts would get access to such benefits? I bet it would! Hiding in our own bubble doesn't serve us as much as we think. That world needs our strengths and talents.

✓ Introverts love having discussions about building a better future and are not afraid to share their opinions

It's well known that introverts prefer silence to small talk. But if they found an interlocutor who resonates at least in part with their big ideas, they're willing to explore the topics further by sharing their personal opinions, building on each other's ideas, and even brainstorming possible solutions.

That's what happened at toward the end of Adina's interview. It felt more like a discussion between two friends than an interview. We both enjoyed that dialog, coming more from a collaborative than confrontational approach—another introvert strength!

List of Introverts' Strengths
covered in this book
gabrielacasineanu.com/list-introverts-strengths

Chapter Nine

LOUISE

Whenever fear is holding you back, work on your passion! Because your passion is going to give you that strength to do the work and to change the things you need to change.

— LOUISE VN LIEBENBERG

We're living on different hemispheres (me in Canada, Louise in South Africa)…but social media helped us connect!

As it was mentioned several times already—social media does help introverts, and not only to connect! I even plan to write a book or create an online course on this topic, so stay tuned! :-)

Louise and I met as members of a Facebook group for authors, both writing our first book. While I was focusing full-time on mine, Louise juggled with more things at the same time: a life skills coaching business, creating art, and a job that complemented her income.

Since introverts are such great observers, we can often hold a mirror to help others see where they are. So, after I'd surprised Louise several times with my remarks, we discovered that we're on the same wavelength on many topics.

At one point she agreed to go through a coaching exercise that I'd suggested, which allowed her intuition to guide her into finding the pen name that suits her best. So I wasn't surprised when—with all her busyness—she found time for this interview, eager to share her journey from a very, very shy introvert to where she is now.

Louise: I think the first challenge I'll share is a problem for all introverts, which is being social—learning how to be social and how to be at ease in the world. I'll tell you how my story started and about my pivotal moment; when things changed for me. I was about 22-years old and was trained as a microbiologist. Although I was very young, I was the head of the microbiology laboratory, so I had to learn how to be a boss, a delegator, and a trainer. All of those things were my second challenge. My first challenge was to be social. I was so shy; so unsure of *how to be* in the world.

I would spend every single moment in the microbiology laboratory—in the deepest, darkest room, which was the room where we worked with tuberculosis slides. I was hiding in that tiny little room in the back, while everybody else went off for tea. "I can't go, I've got too much work!" I would tell them. And I'd go and sit in that little dark room and screen the TB slides rather than go to the tea room. I did this for a long time.

One day, my boss—the chief pathologist—visited our lab. I

didn't see him a lot, so he was quite an intimidating figure for me. He usually didn't have that much interaction with me. This time he called me into his office and he mentioned that he heard from the head of the laboratory that I don't socialize much, and I don't talk to others. And so, I'm sitting there in my chair, and I just want to die! I'm cringing. I don't know where to put my head because I am a perfectionist and I don't like doing anything wrong. And I'm hearing this stuff about myself, this personal stuff!

But I listened. He said to me that it's up to me to reach out to other people. And that I must just start reaching out to one person at a time. To one person, and that's good enough! And I must try to get to the tea room and socialize a bit as people were scared of me. That was hard!!!

So, I crawled out of his office, hid in my deep dark TB room, and bawled my eyes out...I cried and cried. It was so, so, so hard to hear that! But I went back the next day, went into the tea room, and I chatted to the girl next to me. And she became a very good friend. And every single day I pushed myself to go into the tea room. So that's where it started for me. And it was an eye-opener. It was very hard but once I started reaching out to one person, the next one was easier.

I've got to a point where people nowadays will say to me: "At least you're not an introvert"—because I got over it so much. I've also learned that other people are not really about judging you. It's all about being interested in them. And that's how I gradually became a very social introvert.

Another thing I learned about being social is that I've always put this thing on myself that we're supposed to be social. And I've realized that I'm not supposed to be social when I don't want to be! I don't have to be social all the time. I don't have to be like other people. I can take it in the doses that work for me! So, I can be a little bit social, then I can go back and be by myself, recharge and do what I need to do: my thinking, focus to get my creative inspiration... Then—when I'm feeling all filled up again and my introvert self is really well— I can go out again and socialize. But I don't have to do it the way other people do. And there is no wrong or right way to do it! It's just finding a balance, so you're not in your cave the whole time. You need to see people. But you're not only out in the world without taking care of your inner self. So, these are my lessons about being social.

Gabriela: Great, thank you!

Louise: The second challenge started when I'd got that job. Because all of a sudden, I'm supposed to be in charge, delegate, and teach others. I was so scared of people that I could hardly say "You have to do this or do that." So it's been a very, very long learning curve. I can't even pretend that I got it right in that job. I think I've scared people into doing what I want, most of my life. And it's taken a lot of work on limiting beliefs for me, to grow my self-esteem. What was really my biggest challenge—bigger than being an introvert —was being an adult child and having Adult Child Syndrome, which is littered with limiting beliefs.

Gabriela: Please say more about that...

Louise: Adult Child Syndrome is when a child has a difficult upbringing. So what you do is that you learn to be a little adult before you're supposed to. You learn all kinds of coping skills, and you take responsibility for the adults around you. For you, all these coping skills are really survival mechanisms. Then you take it into the adult world, but it doesn't work the same in the adult world. In the adult world, it'll make people go away from you. You're acting as if you're all self-sufficient and in charge, and you never let others see the hurt, scared little child inside you. Because that's how you learned to be as a child to survive. When you add that behavior to being an introvert it's going to make it worse.

I firmly believe that any introvert needs to learn to look at their limiting beliefs and replace them with healthy beliefs, to be easier in the world. That's basically what I've done. I have looked at every single limiting belief that I have found in myself to a point where I'm not willing to play small anymore. Now I'm ready to go into the world to share my message and who I am! And it's been an amazing journey!

Through the whole process, I've learned to become a better leader. It's really easy for me now to explain what I need, and to set really clear boundaries, and to explain consequences, and to be very clear in the workplace on what is expected... Now I really believe that I am worth more and I get excellent support!

Because I addressed my limiting beliefs, I've become better in all areas of my life. I am also an artist. I do pottery and stained glass. I'm more authentic now because I don't have to do my art for other people—I make art for me! And it's been really great for me. Because the more authentic I'm becoming, the more appreciated my art is and more people relate to it. Previously, what I've done for all those years was to make stuff for other people's likes. I'm not doing that anymore! Now I make time to do things I relate to! So, that's my second thing—limiting beliefs!

Gabriela: Quite interesting!

Louise: I have another one for you. I was scared to death of public speaking. And you know, with public speaking…all the other stuff that comes from it: fear of photos, fear of doing videos, fear of being with more than two people at a time, fear of telling my story, and fear of being in groups.

How I managed to get over it? Finding something that I believe in 100 percent! I found a passion and it's bigger than me. And because I found a passion that's bigger than me, I am willing to get up on the stage and speak in front of a thousand people. I can do a TEDx talk, I don't know if I would even put makeup on. That's how strongly I believe in my passion! So, my tip number three would be: whenever fear is holding you back, work on your passion! Because your passion is going to give you that strength to do the work and to change the things you need to change. So that you can get over yourself and get out there to share your unique gifts with the world! Because we all have unique gifts!

We don't need to be limited by being an introvert. We can use all our strengths from being an introvert. We've got a lot of strengths! We can just get over ourselves and share our unique perspective and our unique talents with the world. Having a passion is such an amazing, amazing tool to help us overcome our own challenges!

Gabriela: Nice! :-) I like what you said to introverts: "Have a bigger purpose and get out of your way!" My purpose is to build a better world by tapping into introverts' power!

Introverts are drawn to meaningful causes. When you connect with what's meaningful to you, you'll forget about your inhibitions, you'll get that extra boost of energy and motivation to go out there and achieve what you want. What's meaningful is bigger than you, it's something that you want to contribute to or create in the world. That's exactly what you're talking about.

Louise: It is! I told you we're on the same wavelength.

Gabriela: I recently did a presentation about how to write a non-fiction book to boost to your career, and I used my first book as an example, (it had some credibility: it achieved Amazon's bestseller status in nine countries when I published it).

This was a group of 55 coaches, so I also talked about limiting beliefs. When you start writing a book, a lot of limiting beliefs show up. Without realizing it, you're also working on your self-growth, the old stuff comes to the surface!

"What were your challenges, the inner barriers that you had?" someone asked.

I'm like you, I've worked on myself for many years, removing many of my limiting beliefs. So I mentioned that I didn't quite have any, besides thinking of the financial aspect (I didn't have any income during that time). But the thought that pushed me into writing that book was so big, that I couldn't say "No!" I didn't think that English not being my first language would be a problem, nor that I had never written a book before, or that I didn't know how to publish. All I knew was that I had to write that book! So I put myself in the process, focused on writing while learning about self-publishing…and 10 months later the book was out! That's exactly what you're saying.

Louise: And I have exactly the same challenges as you. I'm also writing in my second language, and it's such a learning curve. I'm still doing another job because I have to pay bills, and I've had all these health challenges. But you know what? Writing and sharing my story and transformative lessons is a bigger thing! And that bigger thing makes me wake up at five in the morning!

Gabriela: Oh, but you have to take care of your health! Because it's important to achieve your dream, your goals, your vision!

Louise: Yesterday was my day off and I said to my husband: "You know what? We actually need to leave. Because if I sit here I'll be editing my book for the whole day." I had to leave, to stay away from my book...otherwise, since I know that it has to be edited, I'll force myself to do it! And I saw the consequences to my health if I force myself that way.

I also realized that I can't do any of this stuff if I'm not 100 percent at my best. So once again, it's the passion that's forcing me to take care of myself.

Gabriela: So your passion is also your best teacher! :-)

Some of the introvert strengths I noticed in Louise' stories:

✓ Once a *tool* is learned, introverts can perfect it

Introverts are not always comfortable in front of authority figures, but that actually helped Louise! Although for a very shy introvert, like she was at that time, it was quite painful.

Pushed by her manager, Louise learned a new *tool*: how to socialize...with one person at a time! When she realized that's not as hard as she thought, and not willing to disappoint her boss, she started to improve the *tool* by using it again and again. In time, Louise noticed that socializing is actually a good thing—even for an introvert! By persevering, it became second nature and eased her into the world.

✓ Introverts notice the gap between self-perception and reality

Through self-reflection, Louise became aware that her perception (*she had to be social*) is actually a self-imposed belief, not a real need (*she doesn't have to be that way all the time*).

Once she noticed the gap, Louise was able to remove the pressure she put on herself. She even designed a process that suits well her introversion: Be a little social > Go back to be by herself > Recharge > Think, focus on getting creative inspiration > When filled up and feel well, go out and socialize! Rinse and repeat! :-)

✓ Introverts are willing to improve their self-esteem and build up their skills

Having a challenging job for an introvert of her age—which required leadership, delegation and training—didn't make Louise give up. Working on her limiting beliefs improved her self-esteem and work performance. She became a better leader, was able to set clear boundaries (what she expects from others, what she accepts), and get support.

✓ Introverts are interested in understanding the human psyche

Being very good observers of their inner world and social interactions make introverts also interested in understanding more about human behavior and what drives it.

That led Louise to take a closer look at her childhood struggles, discovering the Adult Child Syndrome she developed at an early age and how it affected her adult life. Then she took on a more challenging task: to identify and remove the limiting beliefs developed through her difficult upbringing.

Replacing these beliefs with more empowering ones had a positive effect on her adult life, developing her interest to become a life skills coach so she can help others too.

Louise's story brought up another interesting point: on top of the inherent struggles that introverts face due to their personality traits, childhood traumas add another layer that can affect their adult life if they're not healed.

✓ Identifying their passion gives introverts the courage to share it with the world

We already had some examples in the previous interviews.

Did you notice Louise's confidence while she mentioned how open she is now to share her passion with the world? *I am willing to get up on the stage and speak in front of a thousand people. I can do a TEDx talk, I don't know if I would even put makeup on.*

Because of the energy she projects while sharing her message, those who'd see her talk might not believe that she's actually an introvert. But that energy comes from inside, from being connected to her passion, not from being an extrovert. That passion will make her lighten up and break through her fear of public speaking, even if she's scared of it. The message she's willing to share is stronger than herself. She feels pushed to get that message out, to share her unique gifts with the world!

A focus shift—from fear to passion, in this case—could make all the difference!

✓ Introverts appreciate the self-discovery journey

Whether triggered by a painful situation or self-imposed, the introverts' self-discovery journey becomes more enjoyable… becoming their strength! The more they enjoy it, the more they'll commit to staying on this path.

Louise certainly appreciates her journey. She likes how it helped her became more authentic, which is also reflected in the relationship with her art—making people appreciate it more.

Louise surrendered to the force and energy brought up by her passion, even if it wakes her up at 5 a.m. to start working. She also realized that taking care of herself is key to becoming her best!

√ Introverts are selective…

…which helps them better manage their energy.

Because of all the self-growth that occurs in their journey, once they start to stand up for themselves they become even more selective. It's a process, after all, helping them to learn how to get out of their own way…so they can share their unique gifts with the world.

Louise is no longer willing to comply with other's requests unless they are aligned with what she wants. And she makes times for things that are important to her!

List of Introverts' Strengths
covered in this book
gabrielacasineanu.com/list-introverts-strengths

Chapter Ten

PETROS

The most important: I could say that now I get to live in the moment, which I never did before. Since I was always in my head, I could never make a connection with people!

— PETROS ESHETU

As the title of one of his books attests, Petros likes to… *jump*! :-) He's the first one who answered my call for these interviews.

Petros is another introvert who keeps *reinventing* himself and reflecting on his struggles, which brings him interesting insights.

You'll get some captivating stories shared by this Ethiopian-American introvert born in Italy, who spent many years in Zimbabwe before starting his life in America at age 22.

You might not guess why he struggled to connect with others and build relationships, what books turned his life around, and why he's so passionate now about coaching.

But you're about to find out…

Petros: If I think about the challenges that I had in the past, and I was able to overcome, they are probably related to family, personal development, and feeling loved.

Gabriela: Let's start with one of them.

Petros: The biggest challenge was connecting with family members, friends, colleagues—I didn't know how to really build relationships. Maybe this is a problem with introverts, I have no idea. I always had the issue of being perfect. I tried to be perfect and it was very stressful because I had to put this mask on every day when I went to work. It's like I have to be someone else. And then I could only be comfortable with my wife when I come home—because she knows how I am, so I'm okay. With everybody else, it was such a challenge! It was only two years ago when I was finally able to overcome it. I'd got a new job and—unfortunately for an introvert—this was like the worst job! I was constantly meeting lots of people, communicating by email, phone… I had to be with so many people that I didn't know to build relationships…that in the end, I couldn't wear that mask anymore, it was just too stressful! But once I read the Brené Brown's book *The Gifts of Imperfection*, that was the first time I could actually let go. I guess, in my case, it was the shame of being myself. Once I realized that it was a shame and that I could actually be whoever I want and it's ok to make a mistake, I think that's when I let go. So it was definitely about loving myself!

Gabriela: What exactly was it in that book that captured your attention and helped you make the shift?

Petros: I think—if more than anything—it just gave me the awareness that I was not being me! And when she talks about the shame of guilt...I remember once I was with some guys and I noticed my feelings but I didn't know how to process them. I didn't know that was guilt! I thought *I'm just a little different today*...and every day. But there was that shame of guilt, of trying to be perfect! And reading the other stories from Brené's book, that I could relate to, made me realize that I wasn't myself. And once I realized that, everything changed! I still hated the job and I eventually left, but I realized that I can just be myself.

Gabriela: Great!

Petros: Brené Brown has a couple of books, and they all have been huge in raising my awareness. In her book *The Gifts of Imperfection: Let Go of Who You Think You're Supposed to Be and Embrace Who You Are,* she talks about shame from both the male perspective (always trying to know everything), then she talks about the female perspective (always trying to be beautiful), and that shame. So she talks about both, pretty interesting! That was a game changer for me!

Gabriela: Wow, quite powerful!

You said that you put on a mask. What kind of mask was it?

Petros: It was a mask of trying to blend in and not stand out. I realized where this was coming from only when I was writing my first book, and I started to notice all the feelings I had. When I was a kid I was fat, really fat. It was in an African country. It doesn't take much to be fat, but if you stick out the others are going to make fun of you. So I started associating pain with standing out. And I took that with me all these years. I never wanted to be a leader, I never wanted to be in a way that I stick out. So if I have to wear the same clothes as the other people next to me, I will just try to fit in as best as possible, because I assumed I knew what would happen. And that's where the mask was always building for years: *Don't stick out, "Don't be yourself, Be like everyone else and try to blend in!* So, that was a mask I was wearing.

Gabriela: It's such an important topic, I think. Many people might not even realize they're wearing a mask. And I'm happy that you became aware of this at one point, and you were able to overcome it. Congratulations!

Petros: Thank you!

Gabriela: How does it feel now, after you were able to see the other side?

Petros: Oh man, it's just so good! A part of me is angry that I let it go that far, but at the same time, I'm glad I realized it. It's like now I'm only starting to learn about myself! Like: Okay, I don't like doing this type of activity, and I don't like this kind of people. I'm not talking about extroverts, just about certain people within a group I used to be a part of. But the most important: I could say that now I get to live in the moment—which I never did before! You know, I was always in my head. When I met people I used to get like a panic attack or get scared even to just walk out…because I was always in my head saying: *Oh, they're not going to like me. They're going to reject me.* Since that was always in my head, I could never make a connection with people; because they could see that I was scared or think that I don't want or I'm rude (which I'm not). But just being in the moment— that was one thing that I never got to experience as much as I would have liked in the past!

Gabriela: How is it now? What does *being in the moment* bring you?

Petros: It makes me happy and grateful for just what I have! Before I was always thinking: *I don't have enough of this, I don't have enough of that*...but now I'm happy where I am. If I get anything on top of it, it is just a bonus. It also allows me to take inspired action. Like when I wrote my first book: I thought I couldn't do it, but I wrote it in three months and that was it! And you know, if I was still my scared self I would've started to talk myself out of it. Now it's like…whenever I feel something like: *You should be doing this,* I just go and do it without overthinking. It's very different now when you live in the moment.

Gabriela: That's really great! What's your book about?

Petros: The title is *I Came. I Saw. I Jumped! How I Found My Dream Job and You Can Too!*

You might think it's a career book but actually it's more just sharing my story of how I finally got the chance to get out of finance and entered a new field—which is writing—and how I discovered it. So it's more about my journey: how I realized that finance was actually killing me. And even though doing what I love is not paying as much, at least it's getting me somewhere where I'm happy.

Gabriela: What made you realize that you're not happy in that field?

Petros: I wrote in the book actually: when I was a freshman, I didn't know what I wanted to do. A friend of mine told me to go into finance, and that's what I did. Later on, when I was going through this cycle of *I don't like my job*, I realized why I even got into finance: because one person told me: "Just go do it." I don't know if finance was really for me at the beginning. That's the point when I said: "Well, then what is?" That's when I decided to try something different.

Gabriela: Is interesting how a question can turn things around so much, isn't it?!

Do you want to talk about another challenge you've had and were able to overcome?

Petros: When I was writing my first book, I had a lot of challenges. One of them was that I'm going to expose myself, that was the biggest challenge for me! And then my coach asked: "Who's helping you to write the book? Don't forget to write in the book that you're a coach." And I was like: "Oh, I don't know about that because now people are going to ask me for help and I'm trying to figure myself out." Even working through that was such a challenge, the biggest thing I would say, actually changing your identity...saying that you are now a coach! I think that was probably the biggest challenge for me, just to accept that: you're no more the finance professional and it's okay, you can be a coach too! That identity shift.

Gabriela: Okay. So it's not really about changing but accepting that you're a coach.

Petros: Yeah, exactly. That was a big challenge.

Gabriela: And what introvert strengths helped you to overcome that challenge?

Petros: Probably the biggest one was just breaking down everything into smaller little pieces. Step by step. I cannot, as they say, throw spaghetti on the wall and see what sticks. It's hard for me to do that. But I can just say: "Okay, today all

I'm doing is just one page of writing. Or I'm just going to search the websites and just find one thing, and that's it." It's just breaking down to small things, that's how I've gotten through everything.

Gabriela: Looks like baby steps helped you to move forward.

Petros: Exactly. And just to be honest, just having clarity. Before I didn't know what my direction was, I didn't have a vision, actually. So I just went with whatever job pays higher. But I had no direction, and I learned my lesson from that. Which is why now I have clarity and I know exactly what I want. And because I do, I know how to break down the steps. And I know how to have milestones to know that I'm moving forward. For example, if you're not losing weight you're probably not going in the right direction, or you're not doing better. So, I think it's just breaking down these steps and having the clarity of what you want.

Gabriela: And what helped you to get that clarity?

Petros: Having a coach. The past year, I've had seven coaches: for relationships, life, business... I paid a lot of money! The first coach was a relationship coach. And once I saw the changes in me, and how the relationship changed just because I changed, I realized that coaching is what I've been missing. It gave me a roadmap from here to there. And accountability, I think it is a big one.

Gabriela: It is! I'm thinking that's an interesting twist: you went from being coached (being the client) to helping other coaches to get more clients...it kind of multiplies the effect.

Petros: Exactly. Because I can help one person or group at a time, but if I help other coaches to spread their message with their book, it has a multiplier effect. That's kind of the approach I was thinking.

Gabriela: May I ask what did you get from writing your first book? What were the outcomes?

Petros: It changed a lot of things. I don't know if you've had this, but a lot of family and friends, and people I've never talked to...you reach out to them and nothing happens. And then when I had the book out, I've had more emails than ever before, just like you finally become respected for what you're good at. A lot of the messages were saying: "Oh, I wish I wrote a book. I always wanted to write a book since I was a kid." I know, because I was like that too—I felt like that all these years. So definitely, I got more respect amongst people. I also got to be interviewed on national TV in Ethiopia. It was online, but it was broadcast all over Ethiopia. I did not know that. My mom doesn't even live there, but when she went to visit Ethiopia and she got told by everyone: "Your son's on TV." I didn't even tell her yet. So it was just a crazy thing, she's like: "You didn't tell me you were on TV!" I said: "Oh, I thought it was an online thing. I didn't think we were on national TV." So everything changed in a lot of people. They just come to me saying "I'm inspired..." "I want to do this business..."

Gabriela: So other people changed their perspective about you, and they got inspired. What else?

Petros: More confidence in yourself. I think that was the biggest because, this has been in my *life bucket* list, and I ticked it off!!! Then I could run a business at five, ten million... I didn't think I could do that. What was stopping me? So it just took my confidence to a whole new level I would have never expected.

Gabriela: Great! Do you have anything to add from an introvert's perspective?

Petros: I think one of the biggest challenges of an introvert is getting out of the comfort zone and meeting people. Because part of me doing coaching, I have to take the initiative and introduce myself. I really needed to know myself and connect with people. That's how a business starts: if you really want something and you're clear about it, you're willing to forego what you think is shyness (which is not really). It's being willing to step out to get what your final thing is.

I never had many friends, I never talked a lot, and now— once I'm myself—I'm able to relate better. I think that's important for the coaching business.

Gabriela: What I'm hearing: you are yourself and you're better at relating with people, but you also have clarity, a meaningful objective for yourself. Something that gives you the energy to go out and talk with those people.

Petros: Yes. I think when I realized it's not about me, it's about that other person who might need help, it kind of makes me say: *I shouldn't be selfish. I need to go out and set the example that I want other people to do.* And if that has a ripple effect, for example, I help coaches who will help their own clients, it's even better!

Gabriela: I loved what you just said, that it's not about you. It's about something you want to create in the world and that gives you that energy to go out, to get your clients out of your comfort zone and talk with their potential clients. And that's a powerful one for introverts.

Petros: Oh, yeah. There are so many introverts. My wife, she's an introvert too. She sees me growing but she still likes to stay in her comfort zone. I don't push her. I feel like if I say something she doesn't listen. But if I have somebody else write a book, and say: "Hey, read this book," and she reads it, then she will do it. I feel like there are so many people that aren't going beyond their potential.

Gabriela: That's a challenge, especially with those close to us. I also noticed that many people don't like to be told to do something. They like to discover it themselves. Like you, when you read Brené's book: maybe you heard those ideas somewhere else, but that book resonated with you and helped you make the shift.

Petros: Yeah. You have people who are listening to you, then they'll say: "Okay, maybe I should've listened to my mom or dad or brother."

Gabriela: I've noticed that you're like me, Petros. You went through different phases, and you keep changing and evolving. But not everyone is doing the same or is advancing at the same speed. For those who are close to us, although they notice some of the changes we go through...they still keep in mind how we were. That's where the difference comes from: if they don't evolve at the same speed as us...they might not even understand what we're going through.

Petros: Yes. They just think you're the same. And once they see an achievement, they go: "You're an author?"

Gabriela: Exactly. I saw that when I changed my career from engineering to coaching. They're like: "Oh, yesterday you were an engineer, now you're a coach? Common, give me a break!" But I kept sending my newsletters with articles, and they're like: "Oh, she's talking about interesting things here."

I think that, when there's a direction change, many people who know you are waiting to see first how we're doing. If you're doing well, some will congratulate you, but even less will support you. That's why is important to stay connected with people who are going in the same direction since you all can relate to what you're going through and even support each other.

✓ Introverts are great researchers…of their inner world

Like many introverts, Petros didn't stop at acknowledging his inner struggles—his biggest one being building relationships. He didn't focus his energy on blaming others either. He kept his focus on the inner world, exploring it further to understand where those challenges are coming from.

Petros reflected on his own journey and childhood experiences, read books about self-esteem to understand where his struggles are coming from. He also reached out to a few coaches for help, which gave him a roadmap from where he was to where he'd like to be…and the accountability embedded in the process, to help him stay on track.

This strength, along with collaboration, makes introverts good team players. They always look for improvement in themselves and others.

✓ Introverts like to feel a part of something to blend in

In Petros' case, this characteristic put him on a wrong track due to a painful childhood experience: the children making fun of him for being overweight. It made Petros develop the belief that he always has to be like others in order to be accepted. And this belief led to more emotional pain in his adult life.

Petros' eagerness to perform well on a job (driven more by perfectionism) was perceived as a need to behave as others do, which made him live with a double identity: putting on a *mask* at work (that fit his perception of what's needed), while at home he could relax and be himself. As it often happens, it didn't take him long to realize that he can't continue that way. He was able to remove the *mask* and find more genuine ways to blend in when he wanted to.

The positive side of a willingness to blend in, which I consider a strength: it fuels the introvert's willingness to collaborate, to build something together...instead of feeding controversy and competition (which extroverts like).

√ Introverts complement their unwillingness to talk a lot

As Petros noticed, the position he left required a lot of talking —which was not ideal for an introvert. When he took the time to reflect and discover his passion for writing, he became much more at ease because these characteristics are natural to introverts.

Petros is now using his strengths, happy that he quit a job that required a lot of talking. He's writing, he's devoting himself to a meaningful cause (helping coaches to get their books out to empower more people) and combines marketing with strategic thinking as another tool to serve his cause.

Getting more clarity about what he wants gives him the energy to go out and selectively talk to people, while a perspective shift (it's not about him but about what he wants to create in the world) gave him the power to pursue his dream.

✓ Introverts pay attention to triggers

Petros didn't ignore his "AHA" moments that came from reading Brené Brown's books. Nor the insight about what conditions created that *mask*, nor his discovery that his relationship issues were caused by lack of self-love.

These triggers are like powerful gates for self-discovery and learning! Once acknowledged and explored further, they bring a lot of useful insights—which is definitely a strength to tap into.

✓ Introverts are courageous

For Petros, his courage to shift careers is an outer reflection of the inner shifts he experienced. Several times, he took a leap of faith based on his increased awareness and a meaningful cause he resonated with. That happened when he quit his job in the financial sector, when he started writing books and became an author, then becoming a writing coach and adding marketing to his portfolio.

While looking from outside we call it courage, from the inside it feels more like an inner power pushing you to take bold actions without giving too much thought to how others will perceive this change.

✓ Introverts are not selfish

Besides being willing to help others, this strength also helps introverts to be more detached when it comes to making decisions—which often leads to making better decisions!

Petros' relationship struggles lead to relationship coaching when he realized that he might not be the only one affected. Then, he discovered and enjoyed the benefits of personal development and their positive impact on his relationship.

He also helps his wife to understand the benefits of self-growth by sharing what he learned on his journey. While others might want to impose their beliefs on those around them, Petros is giving her space to find whatever works for her. This attitude helps build a stronger relationship since it doesn't add pressure to the daily interactions. It also shows respect for his wife's choices and opinions.

√ Introverts are open to learning...and not only new information!

I could say that introverts are masters of thinking because they think a lot! But not all the thoughts are useful, as Petros realized.

When he learned to be in the moment, he started to enjoy life more and became more appreciative of what he already had. Pleased by such outcomes, Petros started using this *tool* more often, which positively affected his relationships as well.

Being in moment stops the detrimental train of thoughts that is already playing in your head (as a broken record), allowing you to notice what's going on around you and have a more spontaneous response.

In case you didn't know, being in the moment is a form of meditation and science has proved many other benefits of using it more often.

√ Intuition: a great radar for introverts

While paying attention to the present moment (not to the

future or the past), introverts can get insights and are able to interpret them more accurately.

Some of these insights are nagging you to take action right away, as Petros does now. When he gets that impulse, he takes action…instead of overthinking or ignoring it! And he noticed positive results with his writing, for example, which didn't happen in the past when he used to overthink or ignore such thoughts.

√ Introverts make great planners

Introverts' ability to think strategically leads them to become great at planning as well.

Faced with a totally new project—writing his first book— Petros broke down the whole process into smaller pieces. Then he focused on one step at a time to avoid being over-whelmed until he finished the book.

√ Introverts are quiet leaders

Inspired into action by an inner call, introverts can become leaders and often lead by example. As the Chinese people say, introverts are *quiet leaders* because they lead in a quiet way, inspiring people more with they vision and perseverance than with indoctrination.

Petros was surprised by how many people reached out to him after he published his first book. He didn't even tell his mom that he was featured by the Ethiopian national TV broad-caster. Only when he realized how many people were inspired by his story, Petros realized his impact on others. He inspired others just by following his childhood dream of writing and publishing a book to completion. And, in the process, his confidence increased as a byproduct!

✓ Introverts use self-inquiry as a discovery tool

Introverts are good at asking powerful questions to help others and themselves.

As a self-discovery tool, it helped Petros realize why he got into finance in the first place. Then, since he didn't like what he was doing, he asked himself other questions, which gave him a new insight on what he'd love to do…which started his writing journey!

Many such questions come intuitively to introverts. But they also take into consideration and follow through the ideas that come this way (via their intuition), leading to self-discovery.

✓ Getting more clarity helps the sensitive introvert

Only when Petros understood the cause of his struggles and what he wants, he was able to overcome his fear and panic attacks caused by his high sensitivity.

It also helped him to get out of his comfort zone and write a book, even if he's a private person and his confidence was not too high. He was able to *shut down* his critical inner voice and keep going.

That inner clarity also helped him when he shifted to coaching. By walking the path he really wanted to pursue, Petros found ways around his insecurities—which usually accompany such career shifts.

List of Introverts' Strengths
covered in this book
gabrielacasineanu.com/list-introverts-strengths

Chapter Eleven

LILIANA

Nowadays, when I mentor newcomers to Canada, I tell them to keep an open mind by asking "is there anything else I should consider?" and questioning their own beliefs.

— LILIANA NAKAMURA

I was curious what Liliana would share with us since her name is an interesting combination of Latin and Japanese names. Maybe this is why she seems quite comfortable making big decisions, like moving to other countries— although introverts are not too keen to be in a completely new environment. Or did she rely on her introvert strengths while moving from Argentina to Japan, and from there to Canada?

Anyway, introverts are nice people! When I mentioned to Liliana that I lost the recording with her interview, she offered to send it in a written format. Thank you!

We met through UnstoppableMe, a non-profit association that helps newcomers to Canada to be more successful by becoming...you guessed it...unstoppable! :-) Liliana is the President of this association.

Gabriela: Please tell us about some of the most challenges situations you've been through.

Liliana: I faced some of my most challenging times when I lived in Japan, due to the differences in culture, but it was also the time when I learned the most about myself.

I was born and raised in Buenos Aires, Argentina. Both my parents were Japanese immigrants there. I grew up in a bilingual home, speaking Spanish and Japanese, and received formal education in both languages. I also started learning English at age nine. In university, I studied economics but never really got to use that degree because—thanks to my language skills—I always got jobs using languages. One of those jobs was Scholarship Advisor and Cultural Officer at the Embassy of Japan in Argentina. When I was working there, I got an opportunity to go to Japan to work for a prefectural office. (Note: Japan has *prefectures* instead of provinces or states)

I had visited Japan when I was 11 years old, but this time I went to live and work as an adult, so it was quite a different experience.

My first year there was very challenging, not only because of the typical culture shock that any person moving countries would go through but also due to the expectations that Japanese people had on me because of my physical appearance. Since the Japanese population is very homogeneous, Japanese people often make assumptions that if someone looks Japanese, they must be born there and know all the norms. The society has many tacit norms and customs that people born there follow to a great extent. I suppose it's the same in any country, but the Japanese make a big deal out of things that are not within the norm. There is this popular saying: "The nail that sticks out gets hammered down." Meaning that any deviance from the norm is met with criticism. People would get surprised when I showed emotions or moved my hands when speaking. My Japanese aunts and cousins made comments that my hair was not tidy and my clothes were not what a Japanese woman of my age should wear. At the time I thought it was quite hurtful to focus so much on the differences in style or personality.

I also saw many instances throughout my 12 years in Japan, where services or treatment differ for foreigners, and I had a hard time accepting those practices as *normal*.

To give you a few examples of challenging situations:

A landlord can refuse to rent to a foreigner for the simple fact that the person is a foreigner. When I wanted to rent an apartment, I faced this refusal a few times and felt very offended. It would be somewhat understandable if I didn't speak or read the language, but I know the language enough to be able to read the rental contract and communicate with the landlord if there was a problem. With my job at the government office, I had guarantors working for the prefectural office (government employees are deemed very respectable) but nope! Those landlords didn't consider anything and refused to rent to me just because I wasn't born there.

I was once involved in a situation where I had to go to a police station. One afternoon I was with a couple of friends

—a Peruvian girl and a Brazilian guy—in a department store browsing merchandise. The girl left the store a little early, but somehow the store owner thought that she had stolen something and called the police. So the police came in all of a sudden and asked us (the guy and me) to go to the police station. We went, a bit reluctantly because we didn't know where the girl had gone, and of course, we didn't have the supposedly stolen goods. Anyway, we went to the police station and the guy and I were taken into separate rooms for questioning. Although at first, the police officers were politely asking me what had happened at the store, when they asked me for a piece of ID and I showed them my "Alien Registration Card" (that's what the ID for foreigners is called), their faces and attitudes changed completely. The two officers asked me why I was in Japan, what other offenses I had committed in my life, how often I visited that department store, etc. They also said that I would lose my employment for being an accomplice in a robbery. I don't remember other questions or comments but the whole situation was very upsetting. Even so, I kept my cool throughout the meeting and answered all questions very calmly. In the end, since they didn't have any evidence against us, they let us go. It was all a big misunderstanding. I don't recall exactly but I think the police also checked videotapes and confirmed that nothing had been stolen. However, we never got any apology from the store or the police. This incident was really shocking and that was the point when I thought I didn't want to live in Japan forever.

Gabriela: How did you overcome these challenges?

Liliana: I was very fortunate to meet very supportive people. During my three-year tenure at the government, I had co-workers from different countries (Brazil, US,

Australia, Hong Kong, Mexico), and we would get together outside of work to talk about our experiences, both good and bad. We often compared approaches and common ways of thinking in each of our countries. All of these discussions were great to understand different perspectives and helped me develop a more open mind.

When the police incident happened, I decided to tell my manager. I was a little concerned because in Japan when the police are involved in anything, there are repercussions at work. Especially when the person is detained as a suspect, the police immediately tell the employer, and the person loses their job in most cases. Also, that was one of the comments the police officer made to me. I explained things openly to my manager, a Japanese lady in her 50s, so that she was aware. Even though I was relatively new in that company (less than six months in the job), my manager didn't question anything in my story. She believed me, showed a lot of empathy and gave me reassurance that things would be fine.

Dealing with different types of people (distrusting/unwelcoming versus supportive/open-minded) helped me move forward because I confirmed that not everything is negative or dark all the time. We always learn from problems and situations in life.

Another thing I did at the time was read many books. I especially liked self-help and psychology books. I didn't read those types of books before going to Japan. A friend recommended *Man's Search for Meaning* by Viktor Frankl, and I really liked it. It was the first time I came across the idea of having a purpose in life and being resilient.

Gabriela: What helped you decide to move from Japan to Canada?

Liliana: While in Japan, I completed an MBA from McGill University. A part-time, two-year MBA entirely delivered in Tokyo. I had already decided not to stay in Japan forever, and I didn't want to go back to Argentina. Besides, I had the desire to experience living and working in North America. The exposure to a Canadian university made me consider Canada more strongly. I found that I fulfilled the requirements for the Federal Skilled Worker visa, and I applied. About a year later, I met a Canadian guy who I would get married to. So, everything seemed to pull me to go to Canada next.

When I got my Permanent Residence approved in 2010, I started researching on the Internet by reading forums and different websites. To my surprise, 99 percent of the stories I read were negative! People complaining all over the place about not being able to find a decent job and bearing the expensive cost of living. I emailed a couple of people who I met in Japan and had moved to Toronto, telling them that I wanted to reconnect with them once I landed, but they didn't respond at all. An advisor at McGill Japan told me to be cautious because one of the graduates from the program who moved to Vancouver was working as a store clerk in a souvenir shop for Japanese tourists...a store clerk with an MBA?? Even my Canadian husband didn't want to go back to his own country...! That was because after graduating, he lived in Toronto for a number of years and couldn't get a meaningful job. So, the overview and prospects of finding a professional job appeared very grim!

I still wanted to move to Canada, so I started to PLAN for it.

First of all, I started saving and preparing for different scenarios: both of us in good jobs, only one of us with a stable job, neither of us working, etc. I researched the cost of living and had targets for spending. My husband and I discussed contingencies. We said that we would go back to Japan or check on other countries if we didn't get decent jobs in two years. We were determined on not doing any survival jobs.

I made arrangements to be a remote contractor for my employer in Japan since they were struggling to find my replacement. I would keep doing translations and HR reports as needed. In previous years, I also worked as a freelance translator, so I reconnected with some agencies and told them I would be available for more work.

I checked many job sites and job descriptions to understand what employers in Canada were looking for. I researched possible courses to take in human resources to attain the certification in Ontario. I dedicated a portion of my savings for these.

We landed in Toronto on a snowy day on March 31, 2012. We lived with my in-laws in the Niagara region for about three weeks and then moved to a rented basement in Toronto. My husband got a job quite quickly as an ESL teacher, and I did translations and other freelance work as planned.

In May, while browsing the Internet, I found a bridging program for HR professionals, run by a non-profit organization. I attended some workshops and they provided college courses and an internship. Interestingly enough, all the comments by the counselors were quite focused on the things we did not have. They kept saying we didn't have the right skills, that we gave wrong answers in the mock interviews, the resumes didn't look acceptable, etc. All my peers in the

GABRIELA CASINEANU

sessions were complaining as well…of course, misery loves company, so it was a very discouraging environment. Even though the counselors might have had the best intentions to guide newcomers, and the program itself improved a lot in the next rounds, in my cohort we were not set up for success, especially on the emotional side.

Gabriela: How did you overcome the hurdles you described?

Liliana: Throughout the process of looking for a job, a person who was very supportive and encouraging was my mentor. Despite all the negative views I had heard, my mentor kept encouraging me and helping me move forward.

During that bridging program, I took the approach of not expecting much… I thought: *okay, this is a free service that I get because I am a permanent resident. Canada is still a welcoming country in that sense. I'll be thankful for whatever is beneficial for me, and if something does not seem to fit well, I'll discard it.*

My planning before coming to Canada also worked well. I was not desperate to find a job because I had savings and some income.

One thing I could have done differently is to question things I had heard or read about. I was influenced by the "naysayers" and before moving I tended to think that I would never have a career in Canada. Plus, the advice given by certain counselors was not accurate or appropriate. I heard things like: "don't negotiate salary when you get your first job offer," "at the end of the interview say you're available to start tomorrow," "take any entry-level role that you get an offer for." I know people give advice based on their own experience or knowledge, but when dealing with newcomers, they

192

could be more sensitive and judicious. Nowadays, when I mentor newcomers to Canada, I tell them to keep an open mind by asking: "is there anything else I should consider?" and questioning their own beliefs.

Gabriela: How did the previous experience—moving from Argentina to Japan—help you? Was it harder to move from Japan to Canada?

Liliana: That's a very good question! I learned a lot from my first experience moving internationally from Argentina to Japan. I knew what "culture shock" meant! In my three years working for the government, I attended a few training sessions about culture shock: what it was, how to overcome it, and how to help others overcome it.

For me, moving to Canada was like going back to the Western world that I was more comfortable with. Also, I had visited Canada three times before moving. Although being a tourist versus living in the place are very different things, I had a grasp of how life was in Toronto and where to find what I needed. And of course, being married to a Canadian was helpful in the adaptation process. So, all in all, it was not that hard compared to my first move.

Some of the introvert strengths I noticed in Liliana's interview:

✓ A confident introvert embraces new challenges with enthusiasm

That seemed to be Liliana's case. She was raised in a supportive, bilingual environment by parents who taught her appreciation for both languages *(Japanese and Spanish)* and cultures and supported her in learning a third one *(English)*. These aspects increased Liliana's capacity to quickly adapt to new situations and the confidence in her language skills—which gave her the courage to take on new challenges, accepting the position in another country *(Japan)*. Later on moving again, to Canada.

✓ Introverts can easily identify reference points

The supportive environment she grew up in gave Liliana a reference point for what it means to be appreciated for who you really are. Also, it made her more aware of the cultural norms and behaviors that are associated with different languages.

By adding to the introverts' ability to *read* human behavior beyond the surface—and a curiosity to learn about things like culture shock—made Liliana acutely aware of the gap between her own values and expectations, and Japan's cultural norms and behaviors. The big gap between her *reference point* (the *inner standard* she wants to live by) and the *treatment* she was exposed to in Japan triggered her decision to immigrate to Canada.

✓ Introverts have high values

Honesty, equity, integrity are common values to introverts. Having to deal with distrust and an unwelcoming environment with double standards (for locals and foreigners) fueled Liliana's disappointment. Having a supportive work environment was not enough for Liliana to remain in Japan.

Introverts care so much about such values that living a life in misalignment becomes psychologically hurtful (if not also physical). This could also explain why some introverts become *rebels* or *isolate* themselves: they don't want to obey imposed social norms that go against their values.

Environment plays a huge role in shaping our experiences and beliefs. As Liliana's story shows, there is good news: It's never too late to find an environment that suits you better.

✓ Introverts can make wise decisions in critical situations

Fine observers of both the inner and outside worlds, introverts are capable to keep cool outside…even if they become aware of the huge gap between the possible implications and their inner experience. This helps introverts make wiser decisions in critical situations.

Liliana was capable of managing her emotions in the store incident (which she found really shocking), helping her to deal with that situation with a cool mind in the moment—and even after, when she proactively reached out to her manager to talk about what happened.

✓ Introverts are both strategic and process oriented

Liliana highlighted her decision process regarding her second move (immigration to Canada): she started with an inventory of her strengths and expertise *(Canadian MBA, fluent in three languages, international experience, cross-cultural awareness)*, added her desire *(dreaming of the Western World)*, and what she didn't want *(to go back to Argentina)*. With her goal in mind, she started preparing for this move: she thought of what systems to put in place *(potential income sources for worse case scenarios, for example)*, researched information (what people say about Canada, potential resources, etc.), and anything that could help her to have a smoother transition in the new country.

✓ Introverts are courageous when they know what they want

Going through that decision process helped Liliana clarify what she really wanted at that point in her career and what she could rely on: her strengths and expertise, considering them as resources. This gave her the courage to take this step, even if her research results didn't show a positive image of what she could expect in the new country. That courage also helped her persevere until she found a way to land a good job in a competitive market, as she wanted.

✓ Introverts tap into the power of their mind

There's something else that helped Liliana to overcome the challenging situations she encountered after moving to Canada: gratefulness, finding a positive side of every experience she went through! By keeping her focus on finding something to be grateful for, she didn't allow her mind to shift toward negative thinking (which could lead to depression, making it even more difficult to succeed).

She also trusted an inner sense of knowing that she can make it one way or another, in Canada or elsewhere.

✓ Introverts are avid learners

Liliana's curiosity to learn more about self-growth and personal development shifted her perspective about life challenges, with a direct impact on how she approached and overcame the challenges.

Many successful introverts—billionaires Warren Buffett and Bill Gates, for example—are avid readers.

✓ Introverts have high standards for themselves

With an MBA under her belt, and a willingness to not accept less than she was qualified to do, Liliana pushed herself to keep searching until she found a job corresponding to her expectations. Having a *Plan B* (freelance translations and remote work) gave her some comfort while she continued to look for what she really wanted.

Having a high standard raises the bar and can become a motivating factor if you know how to keep your hope alive and manage the options that you already have, as Liliana did.

√ Introverts are willing to pay it forward

A fine observer of social interactions and their impact, Liliana understood the pitfalls of a system that's not able to prepare newcomers for success. So she dedicated part of her spare time to mentoring newcomers and leading UnstoppableMe.

This strength makes many introverts become more generous.

√ Introverts leverage their learning to build a better future

Reflecting on her previous experience in a foreign country *(Japan)* increased Liliana's resilience. It helped her draw important lessons that paved her path in the new country *(Canada)*.

List of Introverts' Strengths
covered in this book
gabrielacasineanu.com/list-introverts-strengths

Chapter Twelve

GABRIELA

Since I was getting the same reaction every time I reconnected with that thought, I started thinking that's the right thing to do. I felt so at peace with that thought, like I was finally coming home...

— GABRIELA CASINEANU

Now is my...the author's turn! :-) It's easier to say than actually choosing and writing my stories. I totally relate with what the interviewees went through!

I've known Gabriela since she was born, I could say, but I'm not sure that's the truth. It took me years to learn more about myself and that's still a work in progress!

Similar to other interviewees' experiences, the *fog* in my mind started to dissipate a bit—and many pieces began to fall into place—when I found out that I'm an introvert, not a weird person who needs to stay apart because she doesn't quite fit into society's mold! I should also admit that—because I didn't mingle much with others—I was able to stay focused on what I wanted (career change, a new path, self-growth, entrepreneurship, making an impact).

Now let me pass it on to F *(an imaginary interviewer)* to take it from here so I can focus on sharing my stories.

F: If you take a look throughout your life so far, is there a recurring challenge that you noticed?

Gabriela: I think there is one: *misalignment*. That's how I call it now. But in the past, I couldn't quite label it, and most of the time I didn't know how to handle it either.

F: What do you mean by *misalignment?*

Gabriela: Let me talk about *alignment* first, more exactly about how it feels. It's like there is a *vertical axis* that goes through your being and each time you're thinking and doing something that's in alignment with it, you feel good, centered, at peace. It's like you're in alignment with your whole being, you feel in integrity with yourself. So *misalignment* is quite the opposite: it's when you feel confused, worried, scared, not at ease with your decisions…obviously, what you're doing is not in alignment with who you really are!

F: Do you remember when *misalignment* showed up for the first time?

Gabriela: I'm not sure, but I remember it being quite present in my first relationship, which ended up being a 13-year marriage. I kept ignoring that feeling, pushing it often aside, thinking that now I have a duty to fulfill as a wife and mother. But it kept coming back, stronger and stronger, to a point that I could hardly recognize myself and wondering if I should do something about this situation or keep accepting it as is. I was in Romania back then—living the life that the society's norms expected from me—but something inside felt wrong, completely wrong! I felt completely misaligned!

I used to be a smart, happy person who trusted her abilities, curious, willing to learn, adjust and explore…but in time my self-esteem greatly depreciated. I was closing myself up, rarely laughing, often crying, feeling more and more tired physically and mentally.

Then…it happened! He (my then husband) went to the States to visit his relatives, hoping he'd remain there and bring us too (me and our children). But the more days were passing by…the better I start feeling! It was like I was coming back to the true ME…the person who can smile again, be open, confident, positive…

Yet, every letter received from him was sending me straight back into *misalignment* for three or four days…enough time to bounce back…until the next letter arrived. It didn't take me long to understand that the *misalignment* (that "*something is wrong*" feeling) came actually from being married to a man with a completely different belief set and perspective about life. Probably that's where his daily judgment—for everything I did—was coming from: I didn't measure up to his expectations of *normal!* And his behavior was deeply affecting me in time, at a visceral level. So I was living a life completely out of sync with who I really am and what I stand for.

Soon after I realized that, I suddenly got this thought: *I should ask for a divorce!* That was a totally new thought to me, but so liberating!!! Yet, quite out of the norm to the society I was living in at that time!

That thought came with such amazing energy that it instantly lighted me up, putting a big smile on my face, opening my arms like I was going to embrace the whole world! Since I was getting the same reaction every time I reconnected with that thought, I started thinking that's the right thing to do. I felt so at peace with that thought like I was finally coming *home*…in alignment with myself! So I filed for the divorce.

Gradually, I started to get back to my true self, which gave me the power to go through the ups and downs of the divorce. And to trust the future, even if I had no clue what it'd have in store for us! I never regretted taking that leap of faith, although at times it wasn't easy to juggle between work and raising two children. But at least, for the time we were together I was able to help them understand life from my perspective as well. This way they had the point of view of both parents to compare and choose whatever works for them…if any.

F: Have you had any similar experience since? A sudden thought that brings you so much energy and courage, taking you on a totally different path? How would you call such experience: a *sudden realignment*?

Gabriela: Yes, you could call it that. I prefer to call it a *heads-up call* from life, to wake you up because you're not heading in the right direction. Or a *sudden alignment* with your true self, who sent you a very clear message via the intuition. I don't know what's the right *label* for it. But I trust the experience more than being worried if I use the right term. I usually pay attention and follow through on such thoughts, when I get them.

I had several similar experiences since, but the strongest was in 2016. I had a full-time job at that time, plus my coaching business. And that job required me to constantly talk to clients and to do workshops almost daily. Which, for an introvert, is quite a lot! I was already feeling that *misalignment* for a while, but I kept pushing it aside thinking that the full-time job pays my bills and I should stick with it while focusing on growing my business in parallel.

By February though, I was so tired—almost exhausted. I didn't have enough energy to focus on the business side for quite a while. I was having a hard time recovering, even sleeping long hours during the week and on weekends. One day, I asked my manager if there's anything we can change about my role, and she answered with an indifferent voice: "I talk too!"

It felt so insensitive! She certainly didn't talk as much as I had to, and probably had no clue how much energy it takes to do a workshop (holding the attention of the group while talking continuously for two hours)! Plus helping the other clients for the rest of the day! And that was…every day!!!

Hearing her answer felt like the whole world collapsed on me! I guess that's the point when I gave up on the thought that someone could understand what I'm going through and help me somehow.

I continued to do my job, and soon I was asked to take on more workshops (when the department had to implement a new program). With the new overload, on top of an already exhausted body, I started experiencing very strange symptoms. It was like my body took control, leaving me powerless: *That's it! I'm in charge now if you didn't do much to protect your health!*

My voice was the first to give up, I couldn't talk for four months. Meanwhile, other symptoms showed up: anxiety, panic attacks, breathing problems, barely walking, dizziness (had to stop at every step to regain my balance), lack of focus and concentration.

By June, when I went to the family doctor, I already had the *crawling insects* symptom in my left arm…so she sent me straight to Emergency suspecting a heart attack! After my heart was monitored by machines for three hours, the doctor came to share the verdict: "You're allergic to…work! :-) Your body is so stressed out by the workload that it affected your overall health!"

YESSSS!!! I wanted to shout, happy that someone finally understood what I'm going through! But all I could give was a faint smile, my voice was still not there!

During the following months, my family doctor monitored my progress, and I started to feel a bit better. But every time the doctor was giving me another note for my manager—that I can't return to work for the next two weeks—my manager was giving me another dose of stress: "What happens after?" she would say with an irritated voice, "When are you coming back? I don't have anyone to do the workshops!"

"How should I know?! I didn't even know that I'd get here!" I answered at one point. I wished I could yell, but I was still having problems talking. My throat muscles would get so tight, that even after saying a few words I had to stop talking!

I couldn't sustain a conversation. It felt like saying anything would take an enormous amount of energy! That made me realize why we introverts instinctively avoid talking: it takes too much energy, so it depletes our energy faster!

Soon after I finally stood up to my manager, I experienced again that *sudden realignment.* I was starting to worry since my other symptoms were gradually decreasing but my voice problem wasn't. It was already August when, one day, I became curious and asked myself: *What would I do with the rest of my life if I can't talk anymore?* And the very next thought was such a surprising answer: *Write a job search book for introverts!*

Dah! That actually made sense, although I never thought of this before! I had never written a book, but it really seemed to be a great idea: by that time I had over 10 years' experience in helping professionals find jobs and advance their careers. And my approach—applying coaching concepts and techniques to employment counseling—was not only quite unique but efficient! I had plenty of success stories as proof that my strategies work, so why not write a book?! After all, I don't need to talk while writing…and the book could reach more people than I could reach myself even if I could talk normally!

Well, these reasons came after. :-) But the thought of writing that book came with so much energy and enthusiasm…that I couldn't simply ignore it! I already experienced before—several times—that such thoughts are truthful, so I surrendered!

Inspired by that thought—and motivated by its energy—I got the courage to remove any other stress; so I resigned from that job! Imagine my manager's surprise! :-) Then I went to the office, took all my stuff and—while waiting for the streetcar to get back home—I again had that wonderful feeling: an immense joy widely opening my arms…ready to sing like an opera singer: *O Soooole Miooo…*

Well, I sang quietly, I was still not able to sing yet.

What followed? Ten months of writing that book seven to eight hours a day, then self-publishing. It became an international Amazon bestseller in the following days and several times since. It was featured above bestsellers for introverts like Susan Cain's *Quiet,* and Richard N. Bolles' *What Color Is Your Parachute (*for job searching and career advice). The book continues to gain momentum and received the Readers' Favorite 2018 International Book Award…even if it was my first book!

Putting all that aside, writing this book greatly help my recovery: by the time it was out, my burnout signs were nearly gone. No more dizziness, better balance, no more anxiety or panic attacks, my body was much stronger…and my focus and concentration were back to normal! I even got a bonus: I fell in love with writing! :-)

F: I'm curious: what did you learn from this experience?

Gabriela: At least four big lessons!

First of all: I now consider that any burnout is a *heads-up call* because you're not heading in the right direction. If you keep ignoring the feeling of *misalignment,* life pushes you somehow to pay attention and to take the right actions. Obviously, doing daily workshops is the worst job for an introvert! Even if you like what you do—which I did—it's probably a pitfall because it makes you continue although you shouldn't. That's another reason why I kept pushing aside my feeling of *misalignment.* I was helping smart professionals—some very smart—who somehow got stuck into the system or in their own thinking and needed just a small push to get back on their feet. It was rewarding to help them!

But the universe showed me there are other ways to get similar results. Like with that book: I was able to write it in a way that gives the readers a similar experience as being in my workshops. I included experiential exercises that help them better understand where they are, what's missing or not working well, and how to bridge the gap with a customized approach specific to their situation. This is the difference between the traditional job search and my approach: it gives the power back to the job seekers, so they don't feel at the mercy of the system anymore.

The second lesson, which I found quite surprising: when I gave up on me (after hearing the manager's insensitive answer), I actually gave up my power to come out from the situation. And what followed? My morale went down leading to health issues that took me on a downward spiral. Only after I questioned myself—and received that energizing insight about writing the book—I regained access to my power, which came with courage and motivation to take the situation in my hands: resign and take better care of myself. From there on, with my mental health getting better, my physical health started to go on an upward spiral—improving my overall health, gradually getting back to normal.

The third lesson reinforced the fact that not trusting what you feel or not taking appropriate corrective actions can lead you to more troubles! That feeling of *misalignment* is such a powerful sign that you're out of integrity, and there are other paths that could suit you better! Don't get stuck in there—for whatever reasons you think you should—get out of your way so you can unfold the right path for YOU!

The fourth lesson: Trust that the feeling of *alignment* will bring something good—even if sometimes it means taking a leap of faith into the unknown! Trust your intuition, your inner wisdom, especially when you navigate through the *unknown territory!* After all, it's a self-discovery journey. A wonderful one I could say...because the challenges you'll get along the way will be your teachers. If you don't give up on yourself, you'll learn more about yourself in the process, about your strengths, new skills...so you'll walk further on your true path of heart!

Do you expect to find here the introvert strengths I've noticed in *my own* stories? Well, they're not here! :-)

Why?

I had three reasons to not list them:

1. I'll take this as ongoing homework for me since it goes beyond what I shared here. That's a nice challenge to take on! Did I tell you that I love challenges? :-)

2. I'd like **you** to do take a moment and do this exercise: What introvert strengths did you notice in this chapter? After reading the previous chapters, and armed with the **List of Introverts' Strengths**, you should be able to identify some.

3. By doing the above exercise, you'll be ready for what's coming up in the next chapters. :-)

See you there, after you identify at least five of my strengths. But I hope you'll find more. :-)

List of Introverts' Strengths
covered in this book
gabrielacasineanu.com/list-introverts-strengths

MY TAKEAWAYS FROM THESE INTERVIEWS

and from writing this book

I had no idea what I was getting into when I decided to follow the idea of writing this book! I stopped counting how many times I went through these interviews. :-)

When I reviewed each interview for the first time, I became aware of many more aspects that I didn't notice while conducting the interview. At that point, I was too focused on the interview itself and so many things went unnoticed. One of them, probably the most important for me was: I didn't realize how much I resonated with several parts of each interview!

After going through all the stories though, I start noticing more general patterns reflected in these interviews.

And yet, another layer of insights surfaced when I went again through the interviews to extract the points I wanted to highlight in my comments. Summarizing these points and writing these comments about introvert strengths was the most intense and creative part of this book. I won't tell you how many times I wished I didn't commit to writing those comments. :-)

But I stuck with this process because I thought that is was an important part of the experience I wanted you to have with this book. After all, there are many books with stories out there…but how many highlight additional layers of understanding and openly invite you to self-reflection? And that was my intention with this book from the beginning.

I don't know what you've gotten out of these stories so far, but reading them triggered many of my forgotten memories to surface. Most of them were buried deep inside my unconscious mind! And I even got some new tips, tools, and strategies to implement that will make my life easier. Yipeee! :-)

Here are some examples:

• **Mimi**'s health struggles and her perseverance to find a way to survive brought to the surface my past health struggles.

I love, loved, loved…her *Bonus Time* concept! I couldn't stop myself asking: What our world look like if we all would consider that we live on our *Bonus Time*? I certainly believe that the world would be better! Don't you?

Going through Mimi's interview made me realize how similar our stories are at a deeper level. It made me more aware of my stubbornness and perseverance to find ways to regain my health, sometimes going in completely different directions than others would. I once even refused a surgery simply because I had a strong inner knowledge that my body could heal itself if I let it…and I was right! That was a totally new concept compared to what I was brought up to believe.

I also loved the long discussion I had with Mimi! So many interesting things came out of it, others got clarified...it made me realize that I should talk more often with introverts! And I've actually started doing that since. :-)

• **Alex**'s integrity—which led him to quit a comfortable position that was threatening his peace of mind—connected me with several situations when I chose integrity over the comfort zone, without having a clear understanding of what I was getting into. Although the journey that followed wasn't easy, I still enjoyed unfolding my professional path this way and especially the outcomes that showed up so far!

His stories also made me wonder how my life would look now if I'd been as aware of my introverted personality and strengths from as early a stage as he was!

I also started debating with myself: am I as analytical as he is? Probably I am—I certainly used that skill in the past, especially in the technical field—but now I'm more interested in balancing that skill with creativity.

• **Mihaela**'s way of thinking in sensations and images made me realize how much I rely on my capacity to perceive sensations—which is my first reaction to visualization exercises, for example, while others perceive vivid images better. I know *kinesthetic* is my primary learning channel, and I found the information I receive this way is more accurate than my logical thinking. :-)

Visual is my secondary channel, which is another way of non-verbal communication. Mihaela's stories reminded me of a meeting I'd attended in the non-profit sector. When someone asked a question, I offered to draw a flowchart that synthe-sized my answer. "Of course you want to draw a flowchart, you have an engineering background!" someone said. We all laughed at that time, but Mihaela's story made me think: *Did I draw a flowchart because of my engineering background? Or did I choose engineering as my first career path because such non-verbal ways of communication* (Kinesthetic/ drawing, Visual/ flowchart) *suited better my introverted personality?* :-)

• I might be biased, but I was really interested in **Gerard**'s ability to learn and master focused networking to a point that he built a national TV program, from scratch, in a new country, in three years! His story made me realize how much I missed all these years when I constantly avoided any networking opportunity—which would've probably helped me grow my coaching business. Since I became aware of his story, I started opening up more, reaching out and asking for *coffee meetings*. I call them *brainstorming meetings for mutual benefit* since I love brainstorming. See, *re*-framing and re-labeling at work! :-) I even started going to larger events, which I completely avoided before; I was an expert in RSVPing and canceling at the last moment. And you know what? I started getting better with those large events as well. But I love these *brainstorming meetings* that I'm initiating lately—great outcomes come out of them!

• **Carol**'s interview reiterated how far our perception of someone can be from how the person actually is! When I met her several years ago, I was taken away by her confidence and how quickly she thought on her feet. If I knew then what I know now about introverts, I could probably have done a better job in recognizing her introversion: she was in an envi-ronment she loved (Toastmasters) and—because of that—she was able to overcome her shyness and anxiety when it came to public speaking. And the way we connected—right away, building on each other's ideas instead of finding flaws in each other's thinking—would've given me a sign that I'd met another introvert. That would've probably made me connect more often with her, thus realizing how smart she is and her excellent expertise. Which she—the shy and modest introvert —didn't say anything about. Maybe I could've helped her somehow so she wouldn't have had to struggle all these years in a Canadian job market that relies on people speaking up —out loud sometimes—about their expertise. But it's not too late for a *brainstorming* meeting. ;-)

• **Charles**' stories about what helped him become a top sales performer were quite insightful! Although I don't plan to become a top sales professional, I can certainly use some of his tips and approaches to boost my sales. I'll need to go back and take some notes for myself!

What I like about his approach is how consciously he designed his work performance around his strengths as an introvert, and how powerfully he balances his work and quiet time. Another smart introvert who managed to learn from an early age about how he is, and he's constantly building on his strengths…at any phase.

• **Louisa**'s stories made me realize how much I got conditioned—in my childhood—to paying attention to the outside world and disconnect with myself. I was not aware at that time (and many more years after) of my introversion and how to deal with it. I didn't know why I was different, nor how to stand up to my sister who told me daily: "You're stupid!" (just because I wasn't like her, although I had great grades in school). Because of her extroversion, she was easily making friends, sometimes even *stealing* mine. At least, that's how I felt. It took me many years to gather enough confidence to stand up for myself and my ideas in front of her.

I love that Louisa realized her need for quiet time an early age, so she was able to arrange her life around that! Also, that she found the courage to ask! That was another big lesson that I learned not long ago. I became better, but I'm still working on it.

• I found quite useful **Adina**'s concept of using *tools* to help us—introverts—communicate with others! Looking back, I intuitively used this concept without being so aware of it. Writing, for example, is such a tool for communication. *Taking* photographs is another one. I used them in my photo-coaching books (designed before Instagram came around).

But using the *tool* concept more consciously—as Adina does —becomes a very practical way to improve my verbal communication.

How the discussion evolved from personal values to a more universal perspective of what's going on and what's possible, made me realize how much we introverts have in common. And how easily we can get to this type of discussion if…we reach out to each other! Another communication booster for me.

• **Louise**'s transformation from a very shy to an outspoken person (easily perceived as an extrovert), could be surprising at a first glance. But it made sense when we learned about the self-growth she consciously put herself through.

Her stories reminded me of my journey from a shy and sensitive little girl (who start crying when she dropped a pen on the first day of school) to gradually *waking up* my consciousness of self, and the massive self-development I've been through since 2006 (using coaching, going to self-growth workshops, reading books, self-healing, and a daily meditation practice). These brought up many positive changes in both my personal and professional life, including getting more clarity about my passion: *to build a better world by tapping into introverts' power.* This passion influences all my work: the books I write, the brainstorming meetings I initiate, the presentations and workshops I do, and my work to build and strengthen membership-based communities.

• **Petros**' story about the *mask* he learned to wear in his childhood really resonated with me. I used to wear a similar mask. Feeling that I don't have much in common with people around me and intimidated by my sister's constant "You're stupid" comments, I closed myself so much that I couldn't express my emotions anymore. Many people considered me a very serious person, that's how my mask looked. Many years passed by until I learned how to express my emotions again, and I still catch myself sometimes holding them back.

Like Petros, I too needed an external trigger to open up and remove the mask. In my case, it started with a coaching session that made me burst into tears and cry for hours! It felt like something suddenly opened up, allowing many emotions to surface at once! I still had to continue that work, to gradually unleash the other layers that had accumulated in time… until I was able to better express how I really am and feel. What a journey!

• **Liliana**'s confidence in navigating two immigration journeys reiterated the importance of raising children in a supportive and nurturing environment that corresponds to their personality. It brought up memories from raising my children in a marriage that was not quite the ideal environment.

Her stories also made me reflect on my immigration journey. The first time I started the immigration process, I gave up after a few months...not believing that I had what it takes to make it on my own in the new country.

Then, as Liliana did, I took an inventory of my strengths and backed it up with some stories of resilience and a good plan —which gave me more confidence! A powerful vivid dream and a meaningful cause were the last *drops* that I needed to start the immigration process again—even if my knee wasn't fully recovered after being dislocated in a ski accident. I still didn't walk normally when I landed in Canada, but that was the smallest thing I worried about.

My integration into Canada was much smoother than hers since I unconsciously tapped into the power of what is called *strategic networking*. I found out only after that's the right term to use for the approach I used. The funny side: when I started my business in 2006, and I had to network... consciously...I totally resisted it! :-)

Thanks to this book, I found a way to re-frame and re-label *networking,* so I can it use more now...the *introvert's way*! :-)

It's interesting how much clarity you can get about your own journey, and what else you can do just by reading and reflecting on other people's stories, isn't it?

I also found captivating the patterns I've noticed throughout these stories, that's why I talked at the beginning about the Hero's Journey—the *Introvert's Hero's journey!*

These stories seem to me like little pieces of this journey, sometimes we've got several pieces with the same meaning (although they're coming from different stories).

This is how I see the *Introvert's Hero's journey*, after going through these interviews: as an upward spiral.

It starts with our childhood experiences which—along with the beliefs passed on to us by the people we get in touch with and society's norms—shape our belief system from an early stage. And, if it doesn't resonate with who we really are, we start experiencing communications challenges. We might buy into the belief that *verbal communication is very important*, for example. Which makes us (introverts) feel very uncomfortable because we're more skilled in non-verbal communication…and we like to express ourselves verbally only in certain conditions, not anytime, anywhere! Because our brains function differently than extroverts, we need more time to quietly recharge. So many introverts end up isolating themselves or looking for activities that require less direct interaction.

Then, at one point, we start becoming more aware of the gap between our belief system and our true way of being. And we start finding ways—or tools—to reconnect with who we really are. And we become more eager to connect with others in a meaningful way. We deeply crave such connections, and to feel that we're part of something bigger, and we can contribute in one way or another.

While walking this path, we discover more about ourselves and the world. We start to open up a bit at the beginning, then a bit more…and more…

Along the way we get more clarity, we discover what we're passionate about and what our strengths are…

We learn to stand up for ourselves more often, we start believing more in our own ideas and rely more on our strengths and talents…

And we'll get to a point where we want to help others more, to start their own *Hero's Journey* or to collaborate to build a better world!

What do you think?
Do you resonate with this Introvert's *Hero's Journey?*

If you do, where do you think you are on this path?

NOW...YOUR TURN! :-)

So far you've read real stories of 12 introverts, plus the comments about the introvert strengths, and my takeaways from writing this book.

As I mentioned earlier, my intention for writing this book is to give you an experience that goes beyond reading some stories!

How did I do so far?

(Shhh...I'm not done yet!) :-)

Now back to YOU!

Seriously, you don't think that I put so much energy in creating this book to let you off the hook, do you?! :-)

Please have a notebook and pen handy and take a moment to reflect on these questions:

• What was *your experience* reading this book so far?

• With what stories, or part of these stories, did **you resonate**?

• Did this book help you **become more aware** of the introvert's strengths?

• What **memories surfaced** while you were reading this book? Do you see those memories in a **different light** now, based on what you learned from this book?

• Did you **learn something new** about **yourself** just by going through this book? And how you can better approach your own challenges?

Ok, I admit it! It'll take longer than a moment. But I guarantee that it's very useful to answer these questions! You can thank me later. :-)

By detaching from the experience of reading and reflecting upon this experience and the stories, you could get new insights...that wouldn't have surfaced while you focused on reading!

If you read the previous chapter, you probably noticed how much I got out of these stories. And I didn't even share everything I learned and all of my insights!

So PLEASE, pause and reflect on what you've gotten so far from this book, and take notes!

Don't let those insights and memories get out of your sight... again! If you resonated with *something*, it's because there are one or more lessons to be learned from it.

After you've reflected on those questions, I have one more exercise for you:

• Think of one of your biggest challenges so far, one that you've been able to overcome.

• Which of your strengths helped you to overcome that challenge? Dig deep, see what you can come up with. Use the **List of Introverts' Strengths** if you're an introvert and need a reminder.

I challenge you to come up with at **least 20 strengths!** Not because I want to be mean, but the more you think about it...the more strengths you'll find.

If you get to: *That's it. I can't find more,* just put that thought aside and wait for another thought to come. If it's not a strength, put that thought aside too...

Keep playing this game until you come up with at least...15!

See I gave you a range, I'm not so mean. :-)

You've probably guessed why I've asked you to go through the above questions and exercise...but I'll say it anyway.

Reflecting on every experience you go through—good or bad—can expand your awareness about yourself and your life in general. The new insights and lessons you'll learn when applied to future situations will help you embrace challenges with a more powerful approach—instead of going in circles by getting similar challenges because you didn't learn your lessons from the previous ones. And, when you don't learn and apply your lessons, the new challenges are usually bigger than the previous ones. You don't want that, do you?

That's all that I have to say...for now! :-)

But I'll come back with other books, for sure!

If you found this book useful, I invite you to
leave an honest review on Amazon
or send it to me at gabriela.casineanu@gmail.com

amazon

I'd really love to read your review or feedback!
Plus, it could help others to make a more informed decision
if they consider buying this book!

Thank you!
Gabriela

LIST OF CONTRIBUTORS

Mimi Emmanuel, multiple #1 bestselling author

- Queensland, Australia
- Mosaic House *(Mimi's Original Scripture & Inspirational Card House)*
- www.mimiemmanuel.com
- Amazon.com/author/mimiemmanuel

Alex Rascanu, BBA (University of Toronto), MPA - in progress (Dalhousie University)

- Halifax, Nova Scotia, Canada
- www.Rascanu.com
- alex@rascanu.com
- Phone: +1 (782) 234-7130

Mihaela Stamate, B.Sc, RMT

- Cambridge, ON, Canada
- Synergetic Therapies

- SynergeticTherapies.com
- Phone: +1 (519) 841-9887

Gerard Keledjian, BA

- Pickering, ON, Canada
- New Horizons Media
- NewHorizonsMedia.ca
- https://NewCanadians.Tv
- gerard@newhorizonsmedia.ca
- Phone: (1) 416-818-2040

Carol Donohue, BS, M.E, PMP, DTM

Author of *In the Moment • Abdicate Down, Delegate Up? • Interpersonal Communication Workshop*

- Toronto, ON, Canada
- Amazon.com/author/caroldonohue
- CarolDonohue.com
- caroldonohue@outlook.com
- Phone: (1) 416-877-7682

Charles Chen, B. Comm

- Toronto, ON, Canada
- ADP
- charles.jh.chen@gmail.com

L.M. Bauman (Louisa)

Author of *Sword of Peace*

- Southgate, ON, Canada

- LouisaMBaumanAuthor.com
- loubau@gmail.com
- Phone: (1)519-575-8976

Adina Ana Vomisescu, Visual Artist, Montessori Educator

Author of *I am just like you*

- Toronto, ON, Canada
- www.adinaana.com
- http://daag.ca

Louise VN Liebenberg, Counselor, Transformational Coach, International Bestselling Author of *Hamster Wheel Relationships for Women*

- Amazon.com/Louise-VN-Liebenberg/e/B07J1HYF2N
- I-nfinitePotential
- www.i-nfinitepotential.com
- louise@i-nfinitepotential.com

Petros Eshetu, BBA, MBA

Author of *The Introverted Immigrant's* Journey • *I Came. I Saw. I Jumped*

- San Diego, CA,USA
- Amazon.com/author/petroseshetu
- Facebook.com/dreampassionlife
- eshetu.petros@gmail.com

Liliana Nakamura, MBA, CHRP, PMP

- Toronto, ON, Canada
- lilynaka@gmail.com

Gabriela Casineanu, M.Sc, MBA, ORSC

Award-winning and International Bestselling author of *books on improving relationships with yourself, your career, and others*

- Toronto, ON, Canada
- Amazon.com/author/gabrielacasineanu
- GabrielaCasineanu.com
- ThoughtsDesigner.com
- gabriela.casineanu@gmail.com

BIBLIOGRAPHY

• Susan Cain, *Quiet: The Power of Introverts in a World That Can't Stop Talking*, Broadway Books, 2013

• Brené Brown, *The Gifts of Imperfection: Let Go of Who You Think You're Supposed to Be and Embrace Who You Are*, Hazelden Publishing, 2010

• Marti Olsen Laney Psy.D. *The Introvert Advantage: How Quiet People Can Thrive in an Extrovert World*, Workman Publishing Company, 2002

• Laurie Helgoe Ph.D., Sourcebooks, *Introvert Power: Why Your Inner Life Is Your Hidden Strength*, Sourcebooks, 2013

• Elaine N. Aron Ph.D., *The Highly Sensitive Person: How to Thrive When the World Overwhelms You*, Harmony, 1997

• Viktor E. Frankl, *Man's Search for Meaning*, Beacon Press, 2006

• John Rampton, *23 of the Most Amazingly Successful Introverts in History* https://www.inc.com/john-rampton/23-amazingly-successful-introverts-throughout-history.html

• Alex Rascanu's interview with Gabriela Casineanu: https://medium.com/@AlexRascanu/how-to-reach-your-potential-an-interview-with-gabriela-casineanu-b3d5dcc898c8

• Irina Cioaca, Neo-classical Composer, Pianist *Beginning* https://irinacioaca.bandcamp.com/releases *(Gabriela Casineanu's daughter)*

• Immigrant Writers Association http://immigrantwriters.com

• Toastmasters International, https://www.toastmasters.org/

• About *Montessori Method of education*, developed by Dr. Maria Montessori: https://amshq.org/Montessori-Education/Introduction-to-Montessori

• What Type of Introvert Are You? (test) https://yourintroverttype.co.uk/

• Visual, Auditory or Kinesthetic: What's Your Learning Style ? http://martinsburgcollege.edu/visual-auditory-kinesthetic-whats-learning-style/

ABOUT THE AUTHOR

Certified professional coach, award-winning author, and artist, Gabriela Casineanu considers life as a self-discovery journey worth exploring.

Her creative and curious soul didn't care much about the MBA and 18 years experience in the technical field (engineering, IT, quality assurance). It found a way to turn things around, leading to coaching (individuals, teams), training, creative entrepreneurship, artistic expressions, and writing.

Through her purpose-driven coaching practice, Gabriela helped thousands of professionals to advance their careers, and creative entrepreneurs to understand how to use the power of their mind to become more successful.

Her bestselling books help the readers discover how to improve their relationship with themselves, career, and others.

Gabriela loves to creatively combine concepts and techniques from various fields, and is passionate about building a better world by tapping into introverts' power.

She finds strength in nature and loves intuitive painting, nature photography, outdoor activities, visiting sacred places, the Holographic Universe concept, and ...wearing that turquoise ski jacket! :-)

To receive notifications about Gabriela's
upcoming books, news from her author journey,
and special offers:
gabrielacasineanu.com/series

More about Gabriela: GabrielaCasineanu.com

Connect with her:

- gabriela.casineanu@gmail.com
- LinkedIn.com/in/gabrielacasineanu
- Facebook.com/gabrielacasineanu
- Twitter.com/thoughtdesigner
- Instagram.com/thoughtsdesigner

ALSO BY GABRIELA CASINEANU

BOOKS

JOB SEARCH / CAREER SERIES

- Introverts: Leverage Your Strengths for an Effective Job Search *(Readers' Favorite Book Award Winner, International Bestseller)*
- Understanding the Employer's perspective on Hiring
- Job Fairs: How to Get the Most of Your Participation

PHOTO-COACHING SERIES (self-coaching)

To improve your relationship with yourself:

- Meeting With My Self: Self-Coaching Questions That Invite Wisdom In (Book 1) *(International Bestseller, featured in Amazon Prime Program)*

- Meeting With My Self (*Workbook*): Self-Coaching Questions That Invite the Wisdom In
- Rencontre avec soi-même: Outil de communication avec la sagesse intérieure (Book 1, French Edition)
- Întîlnire cu mine însumi: întrebări ce deschid oaza înţelepciunii (Book 1, Romanian Edition)

To improve your relationship with others:

- Navigating the Relationship Landscape (Book 2)
- Relations harmonieuses: Carte routière pour naviguer avec aisance (Photo-Coaching t. 2) (French Edition)
- Dezvoltarea armonioasa a relatiiilor interpersonale: Ghid practic (Photo-Coaching) (Volume 2) (Romanian Edition)

amazon.com/author/gabrielacasineanu

SUBSCRIBE TO GET NOTIFIED

To receive notifications about Gabriela's books and updates:
GabrielaCasineanu.com/series

COACHING, CONSULTING, WORKSHOPS

GabrielaCasineanu.com

BOOK GABRIELA TO SPEAK

GabrielaCasineanu.com/contact

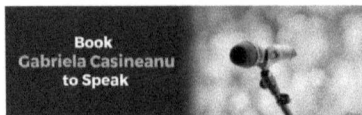

THAT'S IT...FOR NOW! :-)

www.ingramcontent.com/pod-product-compliance
Lightning Source LLC
Chambersburg PA
CBHW031119020426
42333CB00012B/153